LINCOLN CHRISTIAN COLLEGE AND SEMINARY

Series/Number 07-091

NONPARAMETRIC MEASURES OF ASSOCIATION

JEAN DICKINSON GIBBONS
University of Alabama

SAGE PUBLICATIONS
International Educational and Professional Publisher
Newbury Park   London   New Delhi

Copyright © 1993 by Sage Publications, Inc.

All rights reserved. No part of this book may be reproduced or utilized in any form or by any means, electronic or mechanical, including photocopying, recording, or by any information storage and retrieval system, without permission in writing from the publisher.

For information address:

SAGE Publications, Inc.
2455 Teller Road
Newbury Park, California 91320
E-mail: order@sagepub.com

SAGE Publications Ltd.
6 Bonhill Street
London EC2A 4PU
United Kingdom

SAGE Publications India Pvt. Ltd.
M-32 Market
Greater Kailash I
New Delhi 110 048 India

Printed in the United States of America

Gibbons, Jean Dickinson, 1938-
    Nonparametric measures of association / Jean Dickinson Gibbons.
        p.   cm.—(Quantitative applications in the social sciences;
    v. 91)
    Includes bibliographical references.
    ISBN 0-8039-4664-3
    1. Social sciences—Statistical methods.   2. Correlation
(Statistics)   3. Nonparametric statistics.   I. Title.   II. Series:
Sage university papers series. Quantitative applications in the
social sciences; v. 91.
HA31.3.G53   1993
300′.1′51—dc20   93-6480

03 04 10 9 8 7 6 5

Sage Production Editor: Diane S. Foster

When citing a university paper, please use the proper form. Remember to cite the current Sage University Paper series title and include the paper number. One of the following formats can be adapted (depending on the style manual used):

(1) GIBBONS, J. D. (1993) Nonparametric Measures of Association. Sage University Paper series on Quantitative Applications in the Social Sciences, 07-091. Newbury Park, CA: Sage.

OR

(2) Gibbons, J. D. (1993) *Nonparametric measures of association* (Sage University Paper series on Quantitative Applications in the Social Sciences, series no. 07-091). Newbury Park, CA: Sage.

CONTENTS

108020

SERIES EDITOR'S INTRODUCTION

In virtually any research project, a fundamental question concerns the strength of relationships among the variables. How strongly is X related to Y? A common answer comes from calculation of the Pearson product-moment correlation coefficient. However, that calculation implies two necessary assumptions about the variables: a bivariate normal distribution and interval-level measurement.

Suppose, in fact, the variables are ordinal and not bivariate normal. Rather than violating assumptions by application of Pearson's r, the researcher could turn to a distribution-free, nonparametric measure of association. In this carefully written monograph, Dr. Gibbons features Spearman's rho and Kendall's tau, but also presents Goodman and Kruskal's gamma and Somers's d. Which to select? The issue is not trivial, because each generally yields a different numerical value (even if bounded by plus or minus 1). Besides detailed explication of calculation procedures, Dr. Gibbons provides the substantive meaning of each measure. For example, we learn that rho is based on rankings. In contrast, tau is based on paired comparisons, with pairs concordant, discordant, or tied. (And gamma differs from tau_b in the way it deals with ties.)

Of course, the choice of a measure may not depend solely on how it describes the relationship; there are questions of computation and inference as well. Professor Gibbons provides plentiful information on the strengths and weaknesses of leading statistical packages. For instance, she notes that MINITAB does not allow a calculation of tau. Further, she observes that, with SAS, hypothesis tests with tau will be more reliable than with rho. In general, she concludes that the P-values provided by statistical packages for tau and rho are not reliable when the sample size is small. Then special tables, such as those provided in Appendix A, must be used.

So far, only two variables have been assumed. However, relationships among three (or more) variables may be amenable to the nonparametric measure known as Kendall's coefficient of concordance. Or the researcher might wish to control on a third variable—Z—perhaps to test for the possibility of a spurious relationship between X and Y. In this instance, a partial tau could be calculated. Dr. Gibbons spells this out in an artful example on the distraction hypothesis, from Festinger and Maccoby. Here, as elsewhere, the examples are pedagogically powerful. This volume will be extremely helpful to students, teachers, and practitioners of nonparametric methods.

—*Michael S. Lewis-Beck*
Series Editor

NONPARAMETRIC MEASURES OF ASSOCIATION

JEAN DICKINSON GIBBONS
University of Alabama

1. INTRODUCTION

A problem that arises frequently in analyzing data is how to describe the relationship or association between two or more sets of observations, that is, the values of two or more variables. A simple example is the case in which one variable is scores on the Scholastic Aptitude Test (SAT) and the other variable is freshman-year grade point averages (GPAs) for a group of college students, and we want to describe their relationship. Specifically, we would like to know whether SAT scores, which are frequently used as a partial basis for decisions about admission to college, can be regarded as reliable indicators of students' ability to perform in their college course work. If SAT scores are good predictors of successful freshman performance, higher SAT scores will be associated with higher GPAs. If they are not good predictors, there will be no relationship between the two variables.

Measures of association assign a numerical value to the degree of association or strength of relationship between variables. Two variables are said to be *associated* if the behavior of one affects the behavior of the other or, equivalently, if they are not independent. Two variables are said to be *independent* if changes in the value of one variable do not have any effect on the value of the other variable.

Many different kinds of measures of association between two or more variables have been proposed, and their values may need to be interpreted differently. The most commonly known measure of association for two variables is the ordinary correlation coefficient, the complete name for which is the *Pearson product-moment correlation coefficient*. It is calculated as the ratio of the covariance between the two variables to the product of the respective standard deviations. The value of this coefficient always lies between −1 and +1. A nonzero value indicates that there is dependence between the variables. A value of +1 indicates

1

a perfect linear relationship with positive slope, and a value of −1 indicates a perfect linear relationship with negative slope. Further, the square of this correlation coefficient has a specific interpretation in linear regression as the proportion of variation in the dependent variable that is explained by the linear relationship with the independent variable. A value of zero indicates no linear relationship between the two variables (no association). In the case of bivariate normal distributions, a value of zero indicates complete independence between the variables, so that one variable has no effect on the other.

This volume describes and interprets nonparametric measures of association that are appropriate for two or more variables. These measures can be used with variables whose joint distribution is any specified distribution, including the bivariate normal, or whose joint distribution is completely unknown and therefore not specified. For this reason, nonparametric measures of association are sometimes called distribution-free measures of association. All of the measures of association discussed here will require either count data or data measured on only an ordinal scale, as opposed to data measured on an interval or ratio scale. Interval or ratio scale data can always be transformed to counts or ranks, but the reverse is not true. Therefore, these measures are ideal for data that originate as ranks or counts, but they can also be used for measurement data that are transformed to ranks or counts for the purpose of analysis.

The case of two variables is considered first, in Chapter 2, where the procedures based on Spearman's rho and Kendall's tau are covered. Inferences using these measures and applications of these procedures for analysis of time series data are discussed in Chapter 3. The methodology of using Kendall's coefficient of concordance to describe the relationship or agreement among three or more variables is addressed in Chapter 4, and Chapter 5 discusses partial correlation coefficients that measure the relationship between two variables when other variables are held constant so that their effect is eliminated. Chapter 6 describes measures of association for count data in two-way contingency tables with row and column designations that reflect an ordinal level of measurement.

For each procedure included, the rationale behind the descriptive measure of association is described so that interpretation of its value will be very clear. Appropriate techniques of inference are then discussed. Each technique is illustrated by one or more examples of real investigations reported in the recent social or behavioral science literature. The necessary hand calculations are shown in detail for these examples. In many examples the related computer package solutions based on MINITAB, SPSSX, and/or SAS are also provided. Some limitations of these package solutions are indicated when appropriate. The reader who is interested in more detailed information about the nonparametric measures of association described here should refer to the books and articles listed in Appendix B. Many of the books cited in the text and listed in the reference section also contain descriptions of other nonparametric techniques not covered in this volume.

An important caveat in interpreting any measure of association needs to be emphasized. This is that any conclusion that an association exists between two or more variables, no matter how the association is measured, cannot and should not be interpreted as implying a cause-and-effect relationship between the variables. The tendency for people to draw such conclusions is clear, however. A classical example of this occurred when a state raised public school teachers' salaries and later found a high positive correlation between the salary increases and increases in liquor consumption in the state. Critics claimed that the teachers were using their salary increases to purchase more liquor—that is, that the salary increases had caused liquor consumption to increase. However, it is equally logical to argue that increases in liquor consumption caused teachers' salaries to increase. Neither conclusion is justified by the existence of a correlation.

In general, two variables may have an association

1. because they are interacting with each other (i.e., one variable is affecting the other),
2. because of chance or coincidence, or
3. because both variables are affected by other variables that are not included in the analysis.

Case 3 can be investigated by means of partial correlation. Both Cases 2 and 3 are frequently called spurious correlation, meaning false or counterfeit correlation.

2. SPEARMAN'S RHO AND KENDALL'S TAU AS DESCRIPTIVE MEASURES OF ASSOCIATION

This chapter explains how to calculate and interpret two different nonparametric measures of association that describe the relationship between data representing two variables, X and Y. The descriptive measure used in classical statistics is the Pearson product-moment correlation coefficient, calculated as the covariance between the two samples divided by the product of their standard deviations. The two nonparametric measures to be presented here are the Spearman rank correlation coefficient, which is frequently called rho (Greek ρ), and the Kendall tau coefficient, frequently called tau (Greek τ). Both are discussed here because both are used frequently in the social science literature, and readers of this literature who are acquainted with both can better understand what the researchers are doing and can better interpret the meaning of the magnitude of the value of rho or tau in a particular situation.

Both coefficients require a random sample of data pairs (X, Y) measured on at least an ordinal scale and taken from any continuous bivariate distribution. Both have values that range between -1 and $+1$, with absolute values close to 1 indicating a strong association between the variables. A value of zero indicates that the variables are not associated; that is, they have no relationship.

We denote a random sample of n observations from a continuous bivariate distribution by $(X_1, Y_1), (X_2, Y_2), \ldots, (X_n, Y_n)$. The pair (X_i, Y_i) represents observations of X and Y on case i or unit i in the sample, where i ranges from 1 to n. The first step in calculating the *Spearman rank correlation coefficient* is to rank the X elements in the paired sample data from 1 to n and independently rank the Y elements from 1 to n, giving rank 1 to the smallest and rank n to the largest in each case, while keeping the original pairs intact. Hence we end up with pairs $[\text{rank}(X_i), \text{rank}(Y_i)]$. Then we calculate a difference d for each pair as the difference between the ranks of the corresponding X and Y variables. It is always true that the sum of the ds is equal to zero. The test statistic is denoted by r_s and defined as a function of the sum of squares of these differences d. The easiest expression for calculation is

$$r_s = 1 - \frac{6 \sum_{i=1}^{n} d_i^2}{(n^3 - n)} . \tag{2.1}$$

The rationale for this descriptive measure of association is as follows. Suppose that the pairs are arranged so that the X elements are in an ordered array from smallest to largest and therefore the corresponding X ranks are in the natural order as $1, 2, \ldots, n$. If the ranks of the Y elements are in the same natural order, each $d_i = 0$ and we have $\sum d_i^2 = 0$, and substitution in Equation 2.1 shows that the value of r_s is plus one. Therefore $r_s = 1$ describes perfect agreement between the X and Y ranks, or a perfect direct or positive relationship between ranks in the sense that if an X element increases, the corresponding Y element also increases. On the other hand, suppose that the ranks of the Y elements are the complete reverse of the ranks of the X elements so that the rank pairs are $(1, n)$, $(2, n - 1)$, $(3, n - 2)$, . . . , $(n, 1)$. Then it can be shown that $\sum d^2 = n(n^2 - 1)/3 = (n^3 - n)/3$. Substitution of this value in Equation 2.1 shows that the value of r_s is -1. Hence $r_s = -1$ describes a perfect indirect or negative relationship between ranks in the sense that if an X element increases, the corresponding Y element decreases. This might be called perfect disagreement. Both agreement and disagreement are special kinds of associations between two variables. The in-between value, $r_s = 0$, describes no relationship between the ranks of X and Y. In general it can be shown that r_s lies in the range between -1 and 1.

The Spearman rank correlation coefficient can be shown to be equal to the Pearson product-moment correlation coefficient with ranks substituted for the measurement observations (X, Y). Hence if a computer package does not include calculation of Spearman's rho, the original variables can be converted to ranks and the ordinary Pearson correlation calculation then gives the value of Spearman's rho.

Example 2.1

Zellner, Harner, and Adler (1989) report on an experiment to compare persons who have eating disorders with persons without such disorders. Scores of subjects on the Eating Attitudes Survey (EAT) were used to identify persons with abnormal eating behaviors. This survey measures the factors of dieting habits, bingeing and food preoccupation, and self-control. One aspect of the study involved showing the subjects nine figure drawings of women who ranged from very thin (assigned the number 10) to very heavy (assigned the number 90). All subjects were asked to assign to each figure a score as a number between 10 and 90 in intervals of 10 that represented (a) their ideal figure, and (b) the figure they thought was most attractive to males. Suppose that the data in Table 2.1 represent the average over all nine figures of the numbers chosen by a random sample of six women with eating disorders. Describe the relationship between scores on the variables X = Ideal and Y = Attractive using the Spearman rank correlation coefficient.

TABLE 2.1
Average Scores on Nine Figures

Subject	Ideal X	Attractive Y
1	39	23
2	40	30
3	33	25
4	36	32
5	45	40
6	41	35

SOLUTION TO EXAMPLE 2.1: SPEARMAN'S RHO

The first step is to rank the two sets of average scores from 1 to 6 as shown in Table 2.2. Then the differences of these ranks are squared and summed. We substitute $\sum d^2 = 10$ in Equation 2.1 to obtain $r_s = .714$. The agreement between rankings is positive and relatively close to 1, indicating that for these women the figures they consider ideal are similar to those they believe are most attractive to males.

The MINITAB solution to Example 2.1 is shown in Figure 2.1. The package does not include a command for rho, and hence the first command after entering the data into c1 and c2 is to create variables c3 and c4 that represent the ranks of the original variables c1 and c2. Then the correlation command has the computer calculate the Pearson correlation between ranks as .714, which is equal to our Spearman's rho. The SAS solution is given in Figure 2.2. The data need not be ranked for the SAS solution because the package automatically does the rankings in order to calculate rho.

TABLE 2.2
Calculation of r_s

Subject	Ideal X Rank	Attractive Y Rank	d	d^2
1	3	1	2	4
2	4	3	1	1
3	1	2	−1	1
4	2	4	−2	4
5	6	6	0	0
6	5	5	0	0
			0	10

```
MTB >   read Ideal into c1 and Attractive into c2
DATA>   39  23
DATA>   40  30
DATA>   33  25
DATA>   36  32
DATA>   45  40
DATA>   41  35
        6 ROWS READ
MTB >   rank c1 into c3
MTB >   rank c2 into c4
MTB >   name c3='X rank'
MTB >   name c4='Y rank'
MTB >   print c3 c4

 ROW  X rank  Y rank

  1      3       1
  2      4       3
  3      1       2
  4      2       4
  5      6       6
  6      5       5

MTB >   correlation c3 c4

Correlation of X rank and Y rank = 0.714
```

Figure 2.1. MINITAB Solution to Example 2.1

If two or more observations within either the X set or the Y set have the same value, they are called tied. Midranks are assigned to all tied observations. The midrank of a set of tied observations is defined as the average of the ranks they would have been assigned if they were not tied. It can also be calculated as the midrange of the ranks they would have had if they were not tied. When ties are present in the X set or the Y set or both, it is no longer true that r_s can achieve the values -1 or $+1$ even when the relationship is perfect. As a result, we need to make an adjustment or correction for ties. This adjustment is that the formula for r_s in Equation 2.1 is replaced by

$$r_s = \frac{n^3 - n - 6\sum d^2 - 6(t' + u')}{\sqrt{n^3 - n - 12t'}\sqrt{n^3 - n - 12u'}}, \qquad (2.2)$$

8

```
OPTIONS LINESIZE = 80;
CMS FILEDEF RAWIN DISK 2.1    DATA   K;
DATA A;
INFILE RAWIN;
INPUT X Y ;
PROC PRINT;
PROC CORR SPEARMAN KENDALL;
 VAR X Y ;
RUN;
```

```
            OBS     X       Y

             1      39      23
             2      40      30
             3      33      25
             4      36      32
             5      45      40
             6      41      35
```

Correlation Analysis

2 'VAR' Variables: X   Y

Spearman Correlation Coefficients / Prob > |R| under Ho: Rho=0 / N = 6

	X	Y
X	1.00000	0.71429
	0.0	0.1108
Y	0.71429	1.00000
	0.1108	0.0

Kendall Tau b Correlation Coefficients / Prob > |R| under Ho: Rho=0 / N = 6

	X	Y
X	1.00000	0.60000
	0.0	0.0909
Y	0.60000	1.00000
	0.0909	0.0

Figure 2.2. SAS Solution to Example 2.1

where $t' = (\sum t^3 - \sum t)/12$ for t the number of observations tied at any given rank in the X set and the sums $\sum$ are over all sets of t tied X ranks, and similarly $u' = (\sum u^3 - \sum u)/12$ for ties in the Y set. The formula in Equation 2.2 is also equivalent to the Pearson product-moment correlation

TABLE 2.3

Proportion of Coverage of Business Crime

	TV News		Newsmagazines	
Year	Corporate Crime	White-Collar Crime	Corporate Crime	White-Collar Crime
1974	.022	.010	.017	.013
1975	.016	.002	.014	.017
1976	.018	.006	.016	.020
1977	.041	.001	.011	.026
1978	.038	.005	.016	.015
1979	.044	.004	.019	.008
1980	.019	.004	.013	.017
1981	.009	.002	.010	.012
1982	.011	.004	.018	.011
1983	.034	.007	.010	.015
1984	.023	.012	.010	.017

coefficient calculated for the ranks of (X, Y) with midranks used for ties. If there are no ties in either set, $t' = u' = 0$ and the formula for r_s in Equation 2.2 reduces to the expression in Equation 2.1. Example 2.2 illustrates the calculation of rho with this correction for ties.

Example 2.2

Randall (1987) reports a content analysis of TV network news and newsmagazine coverage of business malfeasance over an 11-year period. In this study, business malfeasance was classified as either white-collar or corporate crime. White-collar crimes included insurance fraud, stock fraud, commercial bribery, and embezzlement—that is, crimes that benefit the individual. Corporate crimes were defined as those that benefit the corporation, such as unfair trade practices. For the actual data shown in Table 2.3, the proportions of coverage by TV news were calculated by dividing the average number of seconds devoted to business crime by the total duration of the newscast. The proportions of coverage by newsmagazines were obtained by dividing the average number of column inches devoted to business crime by the total number of column inches available. Randall used Pearson's product-moment correlation coefficient to conclude that space devoted to business crime (a) has declined over time in newsmagazines, but (b) not declined in

10

TABLE 2.4
Data From Table 2.3

Year	TV	X TV Rank	News magazine	Y Newsmagazine Rank	d	d^2
1974	.032	6	.030	6.5	−0.5	0.25
1975	.018	3	.031	8.5	−5.5	30.25
1976	.024	5	.036	10.0	−5.0	25.00
1977	.042	9	.037	11.0	−2.0	4.00
1978	.043	10	.031	8.5	1.5	2.25
1979	.048	11	.027	3.5	7.5	56.25
1980	.023	4	.030	6.5	−2.5	6.25
1981	.011	1	.022	1.0	0.0	0.00
1982	.015	2	.029	5.0	−3.0	9.00
1983	.041	8	.025	2.0	6.0	36.00
1984	.035	7	.027	3.5	3.5	12.25
					0	181.50

TV news, and that (c) the correlation between the amount of space given to business crime on TV news and that in newsmagazines is weak. Verify Randall's third conclusion using Spearman's rho.

SOLUTION TO EXAMPLE 2.2: SPEARMAN'S RHO

Randall's three conclusions do not differentiate between the two types of crime, and therefore the respective proportions for each year can be summed to obtain a single figure for each year as shown in Table 2.4. These figures are then ranked from smallest to largest, with ranks 1 to 11, respectively, and using midranks for ties.

We now need to compute the correction for ties. There are no ties in the X set (TV) and so $t = 0$. For the Y set (newsmagazines) we have three sets of ties (1974 and 1980, 1975 and 1978, 1979 and 1984), each of extent $u = 2$. Thus we find

u	u^3	
2	8	
2	8	
2	8	
6	24	$u' = (24 - 6)/12 = 1.5.$

Substituting these results in Equation 2.2 gives

$$r_s = \frac{11^3 - 11 - 6(181.5) - 6(1.5)}{\sqrt{11^3 - 11 - 0}\sqrt{11^3 - 11 - 12(1.5)}} = .169.$$

The correlation is weak, which confirms Randall's third conclusion, that there is only a slight association between the amount of space given to business crime on TV news and that in newsmagazines.

The MINITAB and SAS solutions to Example 2.2 are shown in Figures 2.3 and 2.4, respectively. The rank command for MINITAB automatically assigns midranks to those observations that are tied. Both solutions incorporate the correction for ties to obtain the same answer for rho as we did.

Another nonparametric measure of association that describes the relationship between two variables is Kendall's tau coefficient. This coefficient is also frequently reported in the social science literature. Like rho, the value of tau ranges between −1 and 1, but tau measures association in a different way from rho.

Specifically, tau measures the association between X and Y as the proportion of concordant pairs minus the proportion of discordant pairs in the samples. Two bivariate observations, (X_i, Y_i) and (X_j, Y_j), are called *concordant* whenever the product $(X_i - X_j)(Y_i - Y_j)$ is positive, that is, when the difference between the X components in the pairs has the same sign as the difference between the Y components in the same pairs. A pair is called *discordant* when the same product is negative. If C is the number of concordant pairs and D is the number of discordant pairs, the Kendall tau coefficient τ is defined as the difference between C and D divided by the total number of pairs $n(n - 1)/2$ or

$$\tau = \frac{2(C - D)}{n(n - 1)} = \frac{2(C - D)}{(n^2 - n)}. \tag{2.3}$$

Hence tau is the proportion of concordant pairs minus the proportion of discordant pairs, or the proportion of pairs that agree minus the proportion of pairs that disagree. The sum $C + D$ always equals $n(n - 1)/2$ if there are no ties, which provides a handy verification of computations.

The easiest way to calculate C and D is first to order the X observations from smallest to largest and list them in a column, and then list the corresponding Y observations in the second column. This makes

```
MTB >   read TV into c1, newsmag into c2
DATA>   0.032 0.03
DATA>   0.018 0.031
DATA>   0.024 0.036
DATA>   0.042 0.037
DATA>   0.043 0.031
DATA>   0.048 0.027
DATA>   0.023 0.03
DATA>   0.011 0.022
DATA>   0.015 0.029
DATA>   0.041 0.025
DATA>   0.035 0.027
        11 ROWS READ
MTB >   rank c1 into c3
MTB >   rank c2 into c4
MTB >   name c3='TV rank'
MTB >   name c4='Mag rank'
MTB >   print c3 c4
```

ROW	TV rank	Mag rank
1	6	6.5
2	3	8.5
3	5	10.0
4	9	11.0
5	10	8.5
6	11	3.5
7	4	6.5
8	1	1.0
9	2	5.0
10	8	2.0
11	7	3.5

```
MTB >   correlation c3-c4
```

Correlation of TV rank and Mag rank = 0.169

Figure 2.3. MINITAB Solution to Example 2.2

$(X_i - X_j) < 0$ for all $i < j$. Then for each Y observation on the list, we count the number of Y observations that are below it and larger than it in the column. The total of these counts is C, the number of pairs of Ys for which $(Y_i - Y_j) < 0$ when $(X_i - X_j) < 0$ for $i < j$. Also for each Y, we count the number of Y observations below it and smaller than it in the column. The total is D, the number of pairs of Ys for which $(Y_i - Y_j) > 0$ when

```
CMS FILEDEF RAWIN DISK 2.2    DATA    K;
DATA A;
INFILE RAWIN;
INPUT   X   Y   ;
PROC PRINT;
PROC CORR SPEARMAN KENDALL;
  VAR    X   Y   ;
RUN;
```

OBS	X	Y
1	0.032	0.030
2	0.018	0.031
3	0.024	0.036
4	0.042	0.037
5	0.043	0.031
6	0.048	0.027
7	0.023	0.030
8	0.011	0.022
9	0.015	0.029
10	0.041	0.025
11	0.035	0.027

Correlation Analysis

2 'VAR' Variables: X   Y

Spearman Correlation Coefficients / Prob > |R| under Ho: Rho=0 / N = 11

	X	Y
X	1.00000	0.16934
	0.0	0.6186
Y	0.16934	1.00000
	0.6186	0.0

Kendall Tau b Correlation Coefficients / Prob > |R| under Ho: Rho=0 / N = 11

	X	Y
X	1.00000	0.11219
	0.0	0.6374
Y	0.11219	1.00000
	0.6374	0.0

Figure 2.4. SAS Solution to Example 2.2

$(X_i - X_j) < 0$ for $i < j$. Then $C - D$ is the difference between the number of concordant pairs and the number of discordant pairs. Observations

14

TABLE 2.5
Calculation of C and D

Subject	Ideal X Rank	Attractive Y Rank	C	D
3	1	2	4	1
4	2	4	2	2
1	3	1	3	0
2	4	3	2	0
6	5	5	1	0
5	6	6	—	—
			12	3

with a tie in either set are called neither concordant nor discordant and are not counted in calculating either C or D. The computation of C and D may be easier if we first rank the X observations and rank the Y observations, but this is not necessary.

The magnitudes of τ are interpreted in exactly the same way as the magnitudes of r_s in the following sense. If the relationship is perfect and positive in the sense that when X increases Y also always increases, all pairs are concordant and $\tau = 1$. If the relationship is perfect and inverse so that when X increases Y always decreases, all pairs are discordant and $\tau = -1$. Note that in either case, the implied existence of a relationship should not be interpreted as evidence of a cause-and-effect relationship between the two variables. The relationship may exist because of many other factors; such a relationship is called *spurious correlation*.

SOLUTION TO EXAMPLE 2.1: KENDALL'S TAU

We compute Kendall's tau statistic for the data given in Example 2.1, reproduced here as Table 2.5. The subjects are rearranged so that the ranks for Ideal X figures are in order from 1 to 6, so we are ready to count the values for the statistics C and D. The first Attractive Y rank is 2. The first entry in the C column is the number of Y ranks that are below 2 and are larger than 2 in the Y rank column, which is 4; the first entry in the D column is the number of Y ranks that are below 2 and are smaller than 2 in the Y rank column, which is 1. We go on to find the sums $C = 12$ and $D = 3$ and substitute in Equation 2.3 to obtain $\tau = .6$, which is again positive and relatively close to 1. Thus the solution based on tau also confirms our previous conclusion based on rho about the relationship between ideal figures and figures attractive to males.

The previously given SAS solution to Example 2.1 (see Figure 2.2) includes a command for calculation of Kendall's tau, and the result given agrees with ours. As yet, the MINITAB package does not include a command for the calculation of tau.

If ties are present in either the X set or the Y set, the maximum value of the absolute value of tau is no longer equal to 1. This is because the ties are not counted in calculating C and D and hence the total number of pairs is no longer equal to $n(n - 1)/2$. Several variations of tau, called tau_a, tau_b, and tau_c, are frequently given by computer packages; these variations provide slightly different treatments of tied observations. The first, called τ_a, simply uses the formula given in Equation 2.3 with no correction. The second, called τ_b, uses the expression

$$\tau_b = \frac{2(C-D)}{\sqrt{n^2 - n - 2t'}\ \sqrt{n^2 - n - 2u'}}, \qquad (2.4)$$

where $t' = (\Sigma t^2 - \Sigma t)/2$ for t the number of observations tied at any given value in the X set and the sums Σ are over all sets of t tied X values; u' represents the same calculation for ties in the Y set. Note that the denominator of τ_b is a function of the geometric mean of the number of untied X pairs and the number of untied Y pairs. The third expression, τ_c, will be discussed in Chapter 6. Below, the calculation of τ_b for the data given in Example 2.2 is illustrated.

SOLUTION TO EXAMPLE 2.2: KENDALL'S TAU

We first reproduce the data from Table 2.4 with the TV set ranks arranged from smallest to largest as shown in Table 2.6. We then calculate C and D, being careful not to count sets of tied ranks as either concordant or discordant.

Tau$_a$ is found from Equation 2.3 as

$$\tau_a = \frac{2(29 - 23)}{11^2 - 11} = .1091$$

and tau$_b$ is found from Equation 2.4 as

$$\tau_b = \frac{2(29 - 23)}{\sqrt{11^2 - 11 - 0}\ \sqrt{11^2 - 11 - 2(3)}} = .1122$$

TABLE 2.6
Calculations From Table 2.4

Year	TV Rank	Newsmagazine Rank	C	D	u	u^2
1981	1	1.0	10	0	2	4
1982	2	5.0	6	3	2	4
1975	3	8.5	2	5	2	4
1980	4	6.5	3	3	6	12
1976	5	10.0	1	5		
1974	6	6.5	2	3		
1984	7	3.5	2	1		
1983	8	2.0	3	0		
1977	9	11.0	0	2		
1978	10	8.5	0	1		
1979	11	3.5				
			29	23		

Note that τ_b is larger than τ_a, as it always will be when there are ties. The previously given SAS solution to Example 2.2 includes a command for calculation of tau. The correction for ties is included and the result given as tau_b agrees exactly with our hand calculations.

3. INFERENCES BASED ON RHO AND TAU

Since r_s and τ are both descriptive measures of association, either can be used as a test statistic for the null hypothesis H_0 that X and Y are independent or have no association. The three possible corresponding alternative hypotheses are as follows:

A_+: positive association
A_-: negative association
A : association exists

The first two alternatives are one-sided, and the subscript on A indicates the direction. The third alternative is two-sided. Note that the conclusion that association exists does not imply that there is either agreement or disagreement between the variables, because there are other kinds of association.

The sampling distribution of r_s under the null hypothesis is given in Table B, Appendix A, for $n \leq 30$; the sampling distribution of τ under H_0 is given in Table C for $n \leq 30$. In both tables the P-values given are in the right tail if the value of the test statistic is positive and in the left tail if the value of the test statistic is negative. For both measures, a small right-tail P-value leads to rejection of H_0 in favor of the alternative A_+, and a small left-tail P-value leads to rejection of H_0 in favor of the alternative A_-. For larger sample sizes, r_s and τ as calculated from Equation 2.1 and Equation 2.3, respectively, are both approximately normally distributed. Under the null hypothesis, both statistics have mean zero; the standard deviation of r_s is $1/\sqrt{n-1}$ and the standard deviation τ is $\sqrt{2(2n+5)}/3\sqrt{n(n-1)}$. This means that the standard normal statistics are, respectively,

$$Z = r_s\sqrt{n-1} \tag{3.1}$$

and

$$Z = 3\tau\sqrt{n(n-1)}/\sqrt{2(2n+5)}, \tag{3.2}$$

and P-values are obtained from the standard normal distribution given in Table A, Appendix A. The Z statistic based on τ approaches normality much faster than the one based on r_s, which implies that approximate P-values for tests based on τ will be more accurate than those for tests based on r_s. It should be noted that when there are no ties, it will generally be true that $|r_s| > |\tau|$ and $|r_s|$ can exceed $|\tau|$ by as much as 50%. The relationship for large n can be expressed as $-1 \leq 3\tau - 2r_s \leq 1$. As a result, inference conclusions based on τ may differ from conclusions based on r_s. This is not unreasonable given that τ and r_s measure association in different ways. The fact that r_s is usually larger than τ does not mean that r_s indicates a stronger relationship than τ. Only the P-values are indicative of the strength of the relationship between variables.

If there are ties in either sample, we use the corrected r_s from Equation 2.2 and the corrected τ_b from Equation 2.4. The exact null distributions of the corrected rho and tau cannot be given in general because the probability values depend on the particular configuration of the ties. If the ties are not extensive, approximate P-values for the corrected rho and tau can still be found from Appendix Table B or Table C, as appropriate, or from Table A, where the corrected r_s and τ_b from Equations 2.2 and 2.4 are used in Equations 3.1 and 3.2, respectively.

18

TABLE 3.1
Data on Children's Scores

Years Behind	Inattentiveness
1.5	4
4.0	24
3.3	9
2.4	44
1.8	36
4.7	29
3.5	11
4.4	42
2.9	31
1.3	26
2.0	39
4.3	14
3.6	48
3.8	54
2.3	46
3.0	51
1.0	17
5.0	21

Example 3.1

Sinclair, Guthrie, and Forness (1984) report on research addressing the claim that attention spans are lower in children with learning disabilities and that consequent inattentiveness leads to underachievement in school. In this study, attention span was measured in the classroom by observing and recording the behavior of each child serially in 6-second intervals in a round-robin fashion until a minimum of one hour of behavior had been observed for each child on each of a minimum of 4 days. Inattentiveness was measured as the percentage of time when behaviors incompatible with assigned task activities were observed. Thus by definition a low attention span is reflected by a high percentage score on inattentiveness. Actual reading achievement was measured by the WRAT test score (which ranges between 1 and 5 years) and then converted to number of years a child lagged behind the appropriate age norm. For the data in Table 3.1 on inattentiveness and "years behind" in reading achievement for 18 learning disabled children in Los Angeles, test to see whether there is a significant positive relationship between years behind and inattentiveness.

TABLE 3.2
Calculation of r_s and τ

X	Y	Rank X	Rank Y	d	d^2	C	D
1.0	17	1	5	−4	16	13	4
1.3	26	2	8	−6	36	10	6
1.5	4	3	1	2	4	15	0
1.8	36	4	11	−7	49	7	7
2.0	39	5	12	−7	49	6	7
2.3	46	6	15	−9	81	3	9
2.4	44	7	14	−7	49	3	8
2.9	31	8	10	−2	4	4	6
3.0	51	9	17	−8	64	1	8
3.3	9	10	2	8	64	8	0
3.5	11	11	3	8	64	7	0
3.6	48	12	16	−4	16	1	5
3.8	54	13	18	−5	25	0	5
4.0	24	14	7	7	49	2	2
4.3	14	15	4	11	121	3	0
4.4	42	16	13	3	9	0	2
4.7	29	17	9	8	64	0	1
5.0	21	18	6	12	144	83	70
				0	908		

SOLUTION TO EXAMPLE 3.1: RHO AND TAU

The null hypothesis is that there is no association and the appropriate alternative to reflect the research hypothesis is A_+: positive association. The first step is to rearrange the data on years behind (X) from smallest to largest, along with the corresponding inattentiveness data (Y), as shown in Table 3.2. Then we rank each entry in the X column from 1 to 18, and similarly for the Y column, and compute the columns labeled d, d^2, C, and D to calculate r_s and τ.

From the values obtained in Table 3.2 we calculate

$$r_s = 1 - \frac{6(908)}{18(323)} = .063, \qquad \tau = \frac{2(83 - 70)}{18(17)} = .085.$$

The right-tail P-values from Appendix Tables B and C, respectively, are both $P > .20$, and so we conclude that there is no significant association between years behind and inattentiveness.

The MINITAB solution to Example 3.1 is shown in Figure 3.1. The result of $r_s = .063$ agrees exactly with ours, but no hypothesis test is carried out. The SAS solution (Figure 3.2) calculates both rho and tau, and the values agree with ours. SAS gives the corresponding two-tailed P-value for tau that is based on the normal approximation to the test statistic given in Equation 3.2. The two-tailed P-value of .62 given by SAS for tau is much closer to the exact value than the two-tailed P-value .80 given for rho because the approximation used by SAS for tau is better than that used for rho. The approximation used for rho by SAS is Student's t distribution with $n - 2$ degrees of freedom and the statistic $t = r_s\sqrt{n - 2}/\sqrt{1 - r_s^2}$. Liebetrau (1983, p. 61) claims that this approximation is not as accurate as ours in Equation 3.1 based on the normal distribution, especially if there are ties.

It is easy to show how the P-values given in Appendix Tables B and C are found when there are no ties. We simply enumerate all $n!$ possible arrangements of $[\text{rank}(X_i), \text{rank}(Y_i)]$ and calculate the corresponding values of r_s and τ for each. Each arrangement is equally likely and occurs with probability $1/n!$. We tally the results and obtain what is called the *sampling distribution* of each statistic. This distribution gives the corresponding P-values for each possible numerical value of r_s and τ. The necessary calculations are shown in Tables 3.3 and 3.4 for $n = 3$.

Because rho and tau both provide a descriptive measure of association and a test of independence or no association, readers may wonder why they need to learn how to use both Kendall's tau and Spearman's rho. One reason, as mentioned before, is that both coefficients appear frequently in the literature and therefore readers of this literature need to understand how they are computed and interpreted. Many statisticians have a preference for Kendall's tau in spite of the fact that Spearman's rho is probably far better known to users of statistics. There are two important reasons for this preference. The first is that Kendall's tau has a very simple and specific interpretation as the proportion of concordant pairs in the sample minus the proportion of discordant pairs in the sample. Spearman's rho has no comparable intuitive interpretation. Both coefficients measure the strength of the relationship between variables, but the definition of the kind of relationship cannot be made precise for Spearman's rho. If Spearman's rho, Kendall's tau, and Pearson's r are each equal to .5, the value .5 needs to be interpreted in three different ways.

A second reason for preferring Kendall's tau over Spearman's rho is that the sampling distribution of Spearman's rho approaches its asymptotic

```
MTB > read X into c1, Y into c2
DATA>   1.5 4
DATA>   4 24
DATA>   3.3 9
DATA>   2.4 44
DATA>   1.8 36
DATA>   4.7 29
DATA>   3.5 11
DATA>   4.4 42
DATA>   2.9 31
DATA>   1.3 26
DATA>   2 39
DATA>   4.3 14
DATA>   3.6 48
DATA>   3.8 54
DATA>   2.3 46
DATA>   3 51
DATA>   1 17
DATA>   5 21
        18 ROWS READ
MTB >   rank c1 into c3
MTB >   rank c2 into c4
MTB >   name c3='rank X'
MTB >   name c4='rank Y'
MTB >   print c3 c4
```

ROW	rank X	rank Y
1	3	1
2	14	7
3	10	2
4	7	14
5	4	11
6	17	9
7	11	3
8	16	13
9	8	10
10	2	8
11	5	12
12	15	4
13	12	16
14	13	18
15	6	15
16	9	17
17	1	5
18	18	6

```
MTB >   correlation c3-c4

Correlation of rank X and rank Y = 0.063
```

Figure 3.1. MINITAB Solution to Example 3.1

```
CMS FILEDEF RAWIN DISK 3.1    DATA    K;
DATA A;
INFILE RAWIN;
INPUT X Y ;
PROC PRINT;
PROC CORR SPEARMAN KENDALL;
 VAR X Y ;
RUN;
```

OBS	X	Y
1	1.5	4
2	4.0	24
3	3.3	9
4	2.4	44
5	1.8	36
6	4.7	29
7	3.5	11
8	4.4	42
9	2.9	31
10	1.3	26
11	2.0	39
12	4.3	14
13	3.6	48
14	3.8	54
15	2.3	46
16	3.0	51
17	1.0	17
18	5.0	21

Correlation Analysis

2 'VAR' Variables: X   Y

Spearman Correlation Coefficients / Prob > |R| under Ho: Rho=0 / N = 18

	X	Y
X	1.00000	0.06295
	0.0	0.8040
Y	0.06295	1.00000
	0.8040	0.0

Kendall Tau b Correlation Coefficients / Prob > |R| under Ho: Rho=0 / N = 18

	X	Y
X	1.00000	0.08497
	0.0	0.6224
Y	0.08497	1.00000
	0.6224	0.0

Figure 3.2. SAS Solution to Example 3.1

TABLE 3.3
Arrangements of Rankings for $n = 3$

X	Y	d	d^2	C	D
(a)					
1	1	0	0	2	0
2	2	0	0	1	0
3	3	0	0		
			$\overline{0}$	$\overline{3}$	$\overline{0}$
	$r_s = 1.00$		$\tau = 1.00$		
(b)					
1	1	0	0	2	0
2	3	-1	1	0	1
3	2	1	1		
			$\overline{2}$	$\overline{2}$	$\overline{1}$
	$r_s = .50$		$\tau = .33$		
(c)					
1	2	-1	1	1	1
2	1	1	1	1	0
3	3	0	0		
			$\overline{2}$	$\overline{2}$	$\overline{1}$
	$r_s = .50$		$\tau = .33$		
(d)					
1	2	-1	1	1	1
2	3	-1	1	0	1
3	1	2	4		
			$\overline{6}$	$\overline{1}$	$\overline{2}$
	$r_s = -.50$		$\tau = -.33$		
(e)					
1	3	-2	4	0	2
2	1	1	1	1	0
3	2	1	1		
			$\overline{6}$	$\overline{1}$	$\overline{2}$
	$r_s = -.50$		$\tau = -.33$		
(f)					
1	3	-2	4	0	2
2	2	0	0	0	1
3	1	2	4		
			$\overline{8}$	$\overline{0}$	$\overline{3}$
	$r_s = -1.00$		$\tau = -1.00$		

normal distribution much more slowly than Kendall's tau approaches its asymptotic normal distribution. This would not be important if extensive exact tables were widely used for small and moderate sample

TABLE 3.4
Calculation of P-Values

r	$Pr(r_s \leq r)$	$Pr(r_s \geq r)$	t	$Pr(\tau \leq t)$	$Pr(\tau \geq t)$
−1.00	1/6	6/6	−1.00	1/6	6/6
−.50	3/6	5/6	−.33	3/6	5/6
.50	5/6	3/6	.33	5/6	3/6
1.00	6/6	1/6	1.00	6/6	1/6

sizes. Exact tables, such as those in Appendix A, should always be used. As noted previously, P-values from the commonly used computer packages are generally not exact and are based on an approximation irrespective of the sample size, and those for tau are more accurate than those for rho.

The tests based on Kendall's tau and Spearman's rho are nonparametric alternatives to the classical test of independence based on the Pearson product-moment correlation coefficient, which requires data measured on at least an interval scale and the assumption of a bivariate normal distribution. The nonparametric tests require data measured on at least an ordinal scale and the assumption of any continuous bivariate distribution, not necessarily the normal distribution.

A measure of the relative effectiveness of two tests to reach correct conclusions in statistical inference is called the *asymptotic relative efficiency* (ARE) and is defined loosely as follows. Suppose we have two tests, A and B, either of which can be used to carry out a test of a specific null hypothesis against a specific alternative hypothesis. The asymptotic relative efficiency of test A relative to test B is the ratio of the sample size required by test B relative to the sample size required by test A in order for both tests to achieve the same power at the same significance level under the same distribution assumptions for large sample sizes.

The asymptotic relative efficiency of these nonparametric tests based on rho and tau relative to the Pearson parametric correlation test is .912 for bivariate normal distributions. This means that the nonparametric test based on a sample of, say, 1,000 observations is as efficient as the parametric test based on 912 observations from the bivariate normal distribution. Thus we have little to lose by using the test based on rho or tau if the distribution is normal. If the distribution is not normal, the tests based on rho or tau may be more efficient than the parametric test.

Kendall's tau and Spearman's rho can also be used in an entirely different kind of inference situation when the data are measurements on a single variable collected at sequential points in time, or time series data. The sequential points in time might be successive years, months, quarters, semesters, training sessions, or the like. Time series data are said to exhibit a positive monotonic trend if the measurements tend to increase in value over time; correspondingly, measurements that decrease over time show a negative monotonic trend. Hence this is like our previous paired sample problem, with X playing the role of time and Y being the measurements.

In general, we let $X_1, X_2, \ldots, X_n$ denote the times of measurement and let $Y_1, Y_2, \ldots, Y_n$ denote the measurements taken at these respective times. The X values here are constants, not variables, and therefore our null hypothesis is different from before. The null hypothesis here is that the Ys are mutually independent and are identically distributed. The one-sided alternatives are as follows:

A_+: positive monotonic trend

A_-: negative monotonic trend

The test statistic is either r_s or τ calculated from Equation 2.1 and Equation 2.3, respectively, or from Equation 2.2 and Equation 2.4 if there are ties. As a result, there will be a significant positive association between X and Y if there is a positive trend; for both statistics the appropriate P-value is in the left tail for the alternative A_- and in the right tail for the alternative A_+. Exact P-values are found in Appendix Tables B and C, respectively. For large sample sizes we use the test statistics calculated from Equation 3.1 or Equation 3.2 and approximate P-values are obtained from Table A.

Example 3.2

Cancian and Ross (1981) report on the changes in media coverage of women over the period of the women's movement in the United States. One aspect of their study concerned the number of items about women covered on the TV evening news by all three major networks combined between 1968 and 1977. The actual data are shown in Table 3.5. Test to see whether there is a significant positive monotonic trend for this period.

TABLE 3.5
Data on Media Coverage

Year	Number of Items
1968	22
1969	18
1970	53
1971	41
1972	68
1973	58
1974	97
1975	192
1976	111
1977	194

TABLE 3.6
Calculations for r_s and τ

	X	Rank X	Rank Y	d	d^2	C	D
1968	22	1	2	−1	1	8	1
1969	18	2	1	1	1	8	0
1970	53	3	4	−1	1	6	1
1971	41	4	3	1	1	6	0
1972	68	5	6	−1	1	4	1
1973	58	6	5	1	1	4	0
1974	97	7	7	0	0	3	0
1975	192	8	9	−1	1	1	1
1976	111	9	8	1	1	1	0
1977	194	10	10	0	0	41	4
					8		

SOLUTION TO EXAMPLE 3.2: RHO AND TAU

We can test the null hypothesis of independence against the alternative of a positive trend by treating these as paired sample data, with X = year and Y = number of items, and use either the Spearman rank correlation or Kendall tau coefficient as a test statistic. The necessary calculations are shown in Table 3.6. Note that for time series data the X values are already ordered.

The test statistics from Equation 2.1 and Equation 2.3, respectively, are

$$r_s = 1 - \frac{6(8)}{10(99)} = .952$$

```
MTB >   read X into c1, Y into c2
DATA>   1968    22
DATA>   1969    18
DATA>   1970    53
DATA>   1971    41
DATA>   1972    68
DATA>   1973    58
DATA>   1974    97
DATA>   1975    192
DATA>   1976    111
DATA>   1977    194
        10 ROWS READ
MTB >   rank c1 into c3
MTB >   rank c2 into c4

MTB >   name c3='rank X'
MTB >   name c4='rank Y'
MTB >   print c3 c4

ROW   Rank X    Rank Y
  1      1         2
  2      2         1
  3      3         4
  4      4         3
  5      5         6
  6      6         5
  7      7         7
  8      8         9
  9      9         8
 10     10        10

MTB > correlation c3-c4

Correlation of rank X and rank Y = 0.952
```

Figure 3.3. MINITAB Solution to Example 3.2

and

$$\tau = \frac{2(41-4)}{10(9)} = .822 \,.$$

The respective right-tail P-values from Appendix Tables B and C with $n = 10$ are .000 and .000 to three decimal places. Therefore we conclude that the data exhibit a strong positive monotonic trend over time ($P < .001$) in amount of media coverage of women.

The MINITAB solution of rho for Example 3.2, shown in Figure 3.3, agrees exactly with our calculation; no hypothesis test is carried out.

```
CMS FILEDEF RAWIN DISK 3.2    DATA    K;
DATA A;
INFILE RAWIN;
INPUT X Y ;
PROC PRINT;
PROC CORR SPEARMAN KENDALL;
 VAR X Y ;
RUN;
```

OBS	X	Y
1	1968	22
2	1969	18
3	1970	53
4	1971	41
5	1972	68
6	1973	58
7	1974	97
8	1975	192
9	1976	111
10	1977	194

Correlation Analysis

2 'VAR' Variables: X   Y

Spearman Correlation Coefficients / Prob > |R| under Ho: Rho=0 / N = 10

	X	Y
X	1.00000	0.95152
	0.0	0.0001
Y	0.95152	1.00000
	0.0001	0.0

Kendall Tau b Correlation Coefficients / Prob > |R| under Ho: Rho=0 / N = 10

	X	Y
X	1.00000	0.82222
	0.0	0.0009
Y	0.82222	1.00000
	0.0009	0.0

Figure 3.4. SAS Solution to Example 3.2

The SAS solution to Example 3.2 (Figure 3.4) gives both rho and tau and the corresponding P-values based on an approximation. Neither of these P-values will generally be very accurate, because our sample size is $n = 10$. As a result, package P-values should not be relied upon when sample sizes are not large. Exact P-values should be obtained by referring the value of the test statistic to the appropriate table, such as those found in Appendix A. The asymptotic relative efficiency of these tests for trend based on rho and tau is about .98 with respect to the test based on the linear regression coefficient when the distribution is normal, and at least .95 for any distribution. The test for trend based on tau is frequently called the Mann test, and the test for trend based on rho is often called the Daniels test.

4. KENDALL'S COEFFICIENT OF CONCORDANCE

In Chapter 2, Spearman's rho and Kendall's tau were developed as descriptive measures of the association between two variables. Now suppose that we have more than two variables—for example, Graduate Record Exam scores broken down into three components (GRE-Verbal, GRE-Quantitative, and GRE-Analytical) for a group of applicants to graduate school. We could use rho or tau to describe the relationship between each of the three possible pairs of variables, but suppose instead that we want to have a single measure that describes the overall relationship among all three variables simultaneously using a single number. In this chapter we will develop such a measure, called *Kendall's coefficient of concordance*. It is the natural extension of Spearman's rho and Kendall's tau coefficients for two variables to measure association between three or more variables.

Suppose we have random samples of n multivariable observations measured on at least an ordinal scale and drawn from any continuous multivariate distribution with $k \geq 3$ variables. Then the procedure is to rank separately each member of the multivariate sample from 1 to n, keeping the original k-tuples intact. Alternatively, the data may be collected in the form of $k \geq 3$ sets of rankings for n objects by k judges. The sums of the ranks given to the respective objects by the k judges are denoted by $R_1, R_2 \ldots, R_n$.

The sum of the ranks for each variable is $1 + 2 + \ldots + n = n(n + 1)/2$, and hence the average rank for each of the n objects is $(n + 1)/2$. If there is no agreement among the judges and the judges assign ranks randomly, each rank for each variable would be the average rank $(n + 1)/2$ and the rank sum for each variable would be equal to $k(n + 1)/2$ because each is the sum of k ranks. The sum of squares of deviations of the actual rank sums around $k(n + 1)/2$ is denoted by S and defined as

$$S = \sum_{i=1}^{n} \left[R_i - \frac{k(n + 1)}{2} \right]^2 . \tag{4.1}$$

On the other hand, if there is complete or perfect agreement among the judges about each of the rankings, each object would have ranks that are all the same and the rank sums would be some permutation of the numbers $1k$, $2k$, $3k$, $\ldots$, nk. The sum of squares of deviations around $k(n + 1)/2$ in this case of perfect agreement is

$$\sum_{i=1}^{n} \left[ik - \frac{k(n + 1)}{2} \right]^2 . \tag{4.2}$$

A relative measure of agreement is then the ratio of the actual sum of squares of deviations between the R_i values and $k(n + 1)/2$, given in Equation 4.1, to the sum of squares of deviations under perfect agreement, given in Equation 4.2. This measure, called Kendall's coefficient of concordance, is denoted by W and defined as

$$W = \frac{\displaystyle\sum_{i=1}^{n} \left[R_i - \frac{k(n + 1)}{2} \right]^2}{\displaystyle\sum_{i=1}^{n} \left[ik - \frac{k(n + 1)}{2} \right]^2} = \frac{12S}{k^2 n(n^2 - 1)} . \tag{4.3}$$

The value of S in Equations 4.1 and 4.3 can be more easily calculated from

$$S = \sum_{i=1}^{n} R_i^2 - k^2 n(n + 1)^2 / 4 . \tag{4.4}$$

The sum of squares of deviations under perfect agreement is the maximum possible value of S and therefore the value of W in Equation 4.3 ranges between 0 and 1, with increasing values reflecting an increasing degree of agreement among the rankings. A value of 0 represents no agreement among the rankings and a value of 1 represents perfect agreement. With three or more rankings, there is no such thing as perfect disagreement. For example, if one ranking is 1 2 3 and a second ranking is 3 2 1, the two rankings are in perfect disagreement. Any other ranking that is in perfect disagreement with the second ranking will be in perfect agreement with the first ranking.

If ties are present in any of the rankings, the maximum value of W is no longer equal to 1. Midranks are used for all ties. The formula for W that incorporates a correction for ties is given by

$$W = \frac{12S}{k^2 n(n^2 - 1) - k\left(\sum t^3 - \sum t\right)}, \qquad (4.5)$$

where t is the number of ties for any given rank by any given judge and the sums $\sum$ are over all sets of ties and all sets of judges. If there are no ties, the formula in Equation 4.5 reduces to that given in Equation 4.3.

Given that W is a descriptive measure of agreement among the rankings, it can also be used as a test statistic for the null hypothesis of no agreement or no association among the rankings. The only possible alternative here is that association or agreement exists among the rankings, and this is expressed as a positive statement, or

A_+: positive association,

because perfect disagreement is not possible with three or more sets of rankings. The appropriate P-value then is in the right tail of the sampling distribution of W or S. Table D in Appendix A gives the right-tail probabilities in the exact null distribution of S for $k \leq 8$ with $n = 3$ and $k \leq 4$ with $n = 4$ and $k = 3$ with $n = 5$ when there are no ties. For larger sample sizes the distribution of

$$Q = 12S/kn(n + 1) = k(n - 1)W \qquad (4.6)$$

is approximately chi-square with $n - 1$ degrees of freedom. Thus the approximate right-tail P-value can be found from a chi-square table such as Table E in Appendix A. If there are ties but they are not extensive, the same tables can be used.

The reader who is familiar with the nonparametric test known as the Friedman test may have noticed that these formulas are identical to those of the Friedman test with k groups and n treatments assigned randomly within each group. This is because the data to be analyzed here are the ranks given by the judges, who are playing the role of the groups in the Friedman situation. The null hypotheses are not the same but the mechanics of the tests are identical.

If we reject the null hypothesis of no agreement between the judges or groups and conclude that agreement exists, we may want to estimate the consensus that is implied by the overall rankings of the n objects. The natural estimate of the consensus ranking is in accordance with the relative magnitudes of $R_1, R_2, \ldots, R_n$. This estimate also has some good statistical properties. First of all, if the Spearman rank correlation coefficient is computed for this estimated set of rankings and each of the k observed sets of rankings, the mean of these k rank correlation coefficients is larger than for any other estimated set of rankings. Second, the sum of squares of deviations between the rank sums for this estimated ranking and what the rank sums would be if all rankings were alike is a minimum over all $n!$ possible estimated rankings. In this sense, this estimated consensus ranking estimate is a least squares estimate.

Example 4.1

Robichaud and Wilson (1976) report on a study of college undergraduates divided into three groups: prejudiced whites (PW), unprejudiced whites (UW), and blacks (B). Each student completed a questionnaire to rate 28 possible goals of social action on a 5-point Likert scale (1 = top priority). The 28 goals were then grouped into five categories, labeled Rights (R) (voting, employment), Integration (I), Self-Help (S-H), Handout (H-O), and Right to Integrate (RTI), and the mean student ratings of importance of the individual goals within each group were computed to obtain the actual data given in Table 4.1. Determine whether there is significant agreement among mean importance ratings for the three groups.

SOLUTION TO EXAMPLE 4.1:
KENDALL'S COEFFICIENT OF CONCORDANCE

The data given in Table 4.1 are the mean importance ratings of $n = 5$ goals (objects) by $k = 3$ groups of students (judges). We first rank the goals from 1 to 5 for each group, as shown in Table 4.2. There are no ties. The rank sums are also given. From Equation 4.1 or 4.4, we

TABLE 4.1

Mean Importance Ratings of Five Types of Goals

	Rights	Integration	Self-Help	Handout	Right to Integrate
PW	2.1	4.4	2.5	3.7	3.9
UW	2.0	3.4	2.5	3.6	3.2
B	1.6	2.7	2.0	2.6	2.2

TABLE 4.2

Three Rankings of Five Types of Goals

	R	I	S-H	H-O	RTI
PW	1	5	2	3	4
UW	1	4	2	5	3
B	1	5	2	4	3
Sum	3	14	6	12	10

calculate $S = 80$ and the P-value from Appendix Table D is $P = .004$. Hence we reject the null hypothesis of no agreement among rankings for the three groups and conclude there is a significant positive association. We can estimate the consensus ranking from highest priority goal to lowest priority goal as Rights, Self-Help, Right to Integrate, Handout, and Integration.

The MINITAB and SPSSX package solutions to Example 4.1 are shown in Figures 4.1 and 4.2. For the MINITAB solution, the first column c1 contains the numbers of the objects to be ranked from 1 to 5, the second column c2 contains the numbers of the judges (groups of students) from 1 to 3, and the third column c3 contains the corresponding data on mean importance ratings from Table 4.1. The command for calculating Kendall's coefficient of concordance is called Friedman because the procedure is equivalent to another nonparametric technique called the Friedman test. The printout shows the rank sums and $S = 10.67$, which is our Q from Equation 4.5. The SPSSX package also gives the numerical value of $W = .8889$ computed from Equation 4.3. Both packages use the chi-square approximation to find a P-value of .031, which in this case is much larger than the exact P-value of .004. Using the asymptotic distribution to find a P-value is not appropriate for such

```
MTB>    read goal into c1, group into c2, data into c3
DATA>   1   1   2.1
DATA>   1   2   2.0
DATA>   1   3   1.6
DATA>   2   1   4.4
DATA>   2   2   3.4
DATA>   2   3   2.7
DATA>   3   1   2.5
DATA>   3   2   2.5
DATA>   3   3   2.0
DATA>   4   1   3.7
DATA>   4   2   3.6
DATA>   4   3   2.6
DATA>   5   1   3.9
DATA>   5   2   3.2
DATA>   5   3   2.2
        15 ROWS READ
MTB>    name c1='Goal'
MTB>    friedman c3 c1 c2
```

Friedman test of C3 by Goal blocked by C2

$S = 10.67$ d.f. $= 4$ $p = 0.031$

Goal	N	Est. Median	Sum of RANKS
R	3	2.0400	3.0
I	3	3.5400	14.0
S-H	3	2.5000	6.0
H-O	3	3.5600	12.0
RTI	3	3.1600	10.0

Grand median $= 2.9600$

Figure 4.1. MINITAB Solution to Example 4.1

small values of n and k. For $k \leq 8$ with $n = 3$ and $k \leq 4$ with $n = 4$ and $k = 3$ with $n = 5$, tables of the exact distribution of S (such as Table D) or W should always be used to find P-values.

The reader may wonder why we did not just calculate Kendall's tau or Spearman's rho for each of the $k(k - 1)/2$ pairs of rankings in the situation of this chapter. We could have done so, but the sampling distribution of the resulting test statistic would have been different from that of S or W. It is interesting to note, however, that if there are no ties W is related to the average $\bar{r}_s$ of the $k(k - 1)/2$ values of r_s by the formula

```
DATA LIST /R 1-3 I 5-7 SH 9-11 HO 13-15 RTI 17-19
npar tests kendall=all
begin data
2.1 4.4 2.5 3.7 3.9
2.0 3.4 2.5 3.6 3.2
1.6 2.7 2.0 2.6 2.2
end data
```

```
- - - - - KENDALL COEFFICIENT OF CONCORDANCE

    MEAN RANK    VARIABLE

       1.00      R
       4.67      I
       2.00      SH
       4.00      HO
       3.33      RTI
    CASES         W      CHI-SQUARE    D.F.    SIGNIFICance
      3         .8889     10.6667        4         .0306
```

Figure 4.2. SPSSX Solution to Example 4.1

$$\bar{r}_s = \frac{kW - 1}{k - 1}. \qquad (4.7)$$

The magnitude of $\bar{r}_s$ ranges between $-1/(k-1)$ and 1, and therefore its value is more difficult to interpret than that of W, which ranges between 0 and 1.

A coefficient W_a that is related to the average $\bar{\tau}$ of the $k(k-1)/2$ values of τ if there are no ties has also been proposed and discussed in Ehrenberg (1952) and Hays (1960). The formula is

$$W_a = \frac{(k-1)\bar{\tau} + 1}{k} \qquad \text{if } k \text{ is even, and}$$

$$W_a = \frac{k\bar{\tau} + 1}{k + 1} \qquad \text{if } k \text{ is odd.} \qquad (4.8)$$

This coefficient ranges between 0 and 1 because the smallest value of $\bar{\tau}$ is $-1/(k-1)$ if k is even, and $-1/k$ if k is odd. The value of W_a is not necessarily equal to that of W, however.

TABLE 4.3
Rank Correlation Coefficients

	PW	UW	B
PW	1		
UW	0.7000	1	
B	0.9000	0.9000	1

TABLE 4.4
Kendall's Tau Coefficients

	PW	UW	B
PW	1		
UW	0.6000	1	
B	0.8000	0.8000	1

For the data in Table 4.1, the reader can verify that the individual rank correlation coefficients and tau coefficients between pairs are as shown in Tables 4.3 and 4.4. The average of the three values of r_s is $\bar{r}_s = .8333$, which is verified by substituting $k = 3$ and $W = .8889$ into Equation 4.7. The average of the three values of tau is $\bar{\tau} = .7333$, which gives $W_a = .800$ when substituted in Equation 4.8 for k odd. We note that W_a is not equal to W here, as is generally the case.

Sometimes the only data given consist of rankings of different groups on several measures. This situation is illustrated by Examples 4.2 and 4.3.

Example 4.2

Humphreys and Smith (1987) report on a study of how well children are able to rank the physical strength of the children in their class. Children in a class were asked to rank all of the class members, including themselves, according to their perception of physical strength, with 1 = weakest, 8 = strongest. For the actual data in Table 4.5 based on a sample of eight 7-year-old boys in a class, (a) use the Kendall coefficient of concordance to test the agreement among rankings and estimate the order of strength of the students, and (b) compute each student's average rank by all other students, find tau and rho as measures

TABLE 4.5
Rankings of Physical Strength

Student Rater	Student Rated (Object of Ranking)							
	1	2	3	4	5	6	7	8
1	5	1	8	3	7	4	2	6
2	4	2	8	3	7	5	1	6
3	4	2	5	3	8	6	1	7
4	4	1	8	2	7	5	3	6
5	4	1	8	3	5	6	2	7
6	5	1	8	3	7	4	2	6
7	3	2	7	4	8	5	1	6
8	4	1	8	2	6	5	3	7
Rank Sum	33	11	60	23	55	40	15	51

of association between those average ranks and each student's ranking of his own strength, and test for positive association.

SOLUTION TO EXAMPLE 4.2(A):
KENDALL'S COEFFICIENT OF CONCORDANCE

For Example 4.2(a), we have rankings of $n = 8$ objects by $k = 8$ judges with rank sums given in the last row of Table 4.5. The value of S from Equation 4.4 is 2,422, and from Equation 4.3 we find $W = .901$, which is close to 1. Appendix Table D does not cover values of k and n this large, so we calculate $Q = 50.46$ from Equation 4.3. We enter Appendix Table E with 7 degrees of freedom and find that the approximate P-value is $P < .001$. Therefore we conclude that there is a significant positive association; that is, there is agreement among the students about their rankings of relative physical strength. We estimate the order of strength, from weakest to strongest, as students 2, 7, 4, 1, 6, 8, 5, 3.

The MINITAB and SPSSX solutions to Example 4.2(a) are shown in Figures 4.3 and 4.4. For the MINITAB solution, column c1 contains the student rated, column c2 contains the student rater, and column c3 contains the respective rankings. As before, the MINITAB command is Friedman and the statistic labeled $S = 50.46$ corresponds to our Q. Both the MINITAB and SPSSX answers to Example 4.2(a) agree exactly with ours because we also used the chi-square approximation to find the P-value. There were no ties here. If there had been, both packages would

38

```
MTB >   read student in c1, student rater in c2, rankings in c3
DATA>   1  1  5
DATA>   1  2  4
DATA>   1  3  4
DATA>   1  4  4
DATA>   1  5  4
DATA>   1  6  5
DATA>   1  7  3
DATA>   1  8  4
DATA>   2  1  1
DATA>   2  2  2
DATA>   2  3  2
DATA>   2  4  1
DATA>   2  5  1
DATA>   2  6  1
DATA>   2  7  2
DATA>   2  8  1
DATA>   3  1  8
DATA>   3  2  8
DATA>   3  3  5
DATA>   3  4  8
DATA>   3  5  8
DATA>   3  6  8
DATA>   3  7  7
DATA>   3  8  8
DATA>   4  1  3
DATA>   4  2  3
DATA>   4  3  3
DATA>   4  4  2
DATA>   4  5  3
DATA>   4  6  3
DATA>   4  7  4
DATA>   4  8  2
DATA>   5  1  7
DATA>   5  2  7
DATA>   5  3  8
DATA>   5  4  7
DATA>   5  5  5
DATA>   5  6  7
DATA>   5  7  8
DATA>   5  8  6
DATA>   6  1  4
DATA>   6  2  5
DATA>   6  3  6
DATA>   6  4  5
DATA>   6  5  6
```

continued

```
DATA>    6 6 4
DATA>    6 7 5
DATA>    6 8 5
DATA>    7 1 3
DATA>    7 2 1
DATA>    7 3 1
DATA>    7 4 3
DATA>    7 5 2
DATA>    7 6 2
DATA>    7 7 1
DATA>    7 8 3
DATA>    8 1 6
DATA>    8 2 6
DATA>    8 3 7
DATA>    8 4 6
DATA>    8 5 7
DATA>    8 6 6
DATA>    8 7 6
DATA>    8 8 7
        64 ROWS READ
MTB >   name c1='Student'
MTB >   friedman c3 c1 c2
```

Friedman test of C3 by Student blocked by C2

$S = 50.46$ d.f. $= 7$ $p = 0.000$

		Est.	Sum of
Student	N	Median	RANKS
1	8	4.172	33.0
2	8	1.172	11.0
3	8	7.984	60.0
4	8	2.797	23.0
5	8	6.984	55.0
6	8	5.047	40.0
7	8	1.922	15.0
8	8	6.297	51.0

Grand median = 4.547

Figure 4.3. MINITAB Solution to Example 4.2(a)

have also given the value of the test statistic with the correction for ties incorporated, and the corresponding P-value.

```
data list /s1 1-2 s2 3-4 s3 5-6 s4 7-8 s5 9-10 s6 11-12
          s7 13-14 s8 15-16
npar tests kendall=all
begin data
5 1 8 3 7 4 2 6
4 2 8 3 7 5 1 6
4 2 5 3 8 6 1 7
4 1 8 2 7 5 3 6
4 1 8 3 5 6 2 7
5 1 8 3 7 4 2 6
3 2 7 4 8 5 1 6
4 1 8 2 6 5 3 7
end data
```

- - - - -Kendall Coefficient of Concordance

Mean Rank	Student
4.13	S1
1.38	S2
7.50	S3
2.88	S4
6.88	S5
5.00	S6
1.88	S7
6.38	S8

0	Cases	W	Chi-Square	D.F.	Significance
	8	.9010	50.4583	7	.0000

Figure 4.4. SPSSX Solution to Example 4.2(a)

SOLUTION TO EXAMPLE 4.2(B):
KENDALL'S TAU AND SPEARMAN'S RHO

For Example 4.2(b) we simply note that each student's ranking of his own strength is the entry in the diagonal position of Table 4.5. For example, student 1 ranked himself as fifth, student 2 ranked himself as second, and so forth. The average rank given to student 1 by all of the other students is the sum of the last seven ranks in column 1 divided by 7, or $28/7 = 4$. The average rank given to student 2 by all the other students is the sum of all numbers in column 2 except for row 2 divided by 7, or $9/7 = 1.3$. We continue in this way to get the pairs of numbers shown in Table 4.6.

TABLE 4.6
Calculations From Table 4.5

Student	1	2	3	4	5	6	7	8
Ranking by self (X)	5	2	5	2	5	4	1	7
Average of others (Y)	4.0	1.3	7.7	3.0	7.1	5.1	2.0	6.3

TABLE 4.7
Calculations for Example 4.2(b)

X Array	Y	X Rank	Y Rank	d^2	C	D	t	t^2	t^3
1	2.0	1	2	1.00	6	1	2	4	8
2	1.3	2.5	1	2.25	5	0	3	9	27
2	3.0	2.5	3	0.25	5	0	5	13	35
4	5.1	4	5	1.00	3	1			
5	4.0	6	4	4.00	1	0			
5	7.7	6	8	4.00	0	1			
5	7.1	6	7	1.00	0	1			
7	7.0	8	6	4.00					
				17.50	20	4			

These pairs must be arrayed by X and separately ranked from 1 to 8, using midranks for ties, as shown in Table 4.7. Then we calculate Spearman's rho and Kendall's tau in the usual way from Equation 2.2 and Equation 2.4, respectively. There are no ties in the Y ranks but there are two sets of ties in the X ranks. These ties affect the calculations of C and D. For example, the C score for Y rank equal to 1 is only 5; the Y rank 3 does not count because the corresponding X ranks are tied. It may be necessary in some cases to list all possible pairs in order to calculate C and D correctly, especially if there are ties in both the X ranks and Y ranks.

$$\tau_b = \frac{2(20-4)}{\sqrt{64-8-2(4)}\ \sqrt{64-8}} = .617$$

$$r_s = \frac{8^3 - 8 - 6(17.50) - 6(2.5)}{\sqrt{8^3 - 8 - 12(2.5)}\ \sqrt{8^3 - 8}} = .786$$

```
MTB >   read c4 c5
DATA>   5 4
DATA>   2 1.3
DATA>   5 7.7
DATA>   2 3
DATA>   5 7.1
DATA>   4 5.1
DATA>   1 2
DATA>   7 6.3
      8 ROWS READ
MTB >   rank c4 into c6
MTB >   rank c5 into c7
MTB >   name c6='X rank'
MTB >   name c7='Y rank'
MTB >   correlation c6 and c7

Correlation of X rank and Y rank = 0.786
```

Figure 4.5. MINITAB Solution to Example 4.2(b)

The right-tail P-value for r_s from Appendix Table B is .014, and the right-tail P-value for τ_b from Table C is between .016 and .031. The association between rankings by self and rankings by others is significant and positive at the .05 level, using either measure.

The MINITAB solution to Example 4.2(b) (Figure 4.5) gives only the value of rho. The SAS solution to Example 4.2(b) (Figure 4.6) shows the values for rho and tau calculated with the corrections for ties, and the results agree with our hand calculations. The two-tailed P-values given are based on an approximation; because the sample size here is $n = 8$, these P-values are not close to the exact values we obtained from Tables B and C. As yet, SPSSX does not include a calculation of tau except for data cast in a contingency table.

The test for independence based on Kendall's coefficient of concordance can be used in a situation where two or more variables are not directly comparable because they use different scales of measurement. For example, suppose a psychologist wants to compare four variables that represent different ways of measuring response to a specified stimulus, using five students as subjects. If variable A is measured on a scale from 0 to 100 and variable B is measured on a scale from 1 to 5, comparison of the relative magnitude of a student's response to variable A with the response to variable B makes no sense. However, if each of the five students is measured on all four variables, the five students can

```
OPTIONS LINESIZE=80;
CMS FILEDEF RAWIN DISK 5  DATA    K;
DATA A;
INFILE RAWIN,
INPUT X Y ;
PROC PRINT;
PROC CORR SPEARMAN KENDALL;
 VAR X Y ;
RUN;
```

```
                OBS    X    Y

                 1     5   4.0
                 2     2   1.3
                 3     5   7.7
                 4     2   3.0
                 5     5   7.1
                 6     4   5.1
                 7     1   2.0
                 8     7   6.3
```

Correlation Analysis

2 'VAR' Variables: X   Y

Spearman Correlation Coefficients / Prob > |R| under Ho: Rho=0 / N = 8

```
                        X              Y

          X         1.00000        0.78565
                    0.0            0.0208


          Y         0.78565        1.00000
                    0.0208         0.0
```

Kendall Tau b Correlation Coefficients / Prob > |R| under Ho: Rho=0 / N = 8

```
                        X              Y

          X         1.00000        0.61721
                    0.0            0.0400


          Y         0.61721        1.00000
                    0.0400         0.0
```

Figure 4.6. SAS Solution to Example 4.2(b)

be compared (ranked) on each variable separately, producing four groups of rankings. Kendall's coefficient of concordance can be used to measure the agreement among these four groups of rankings of students and to test the null hypothesis of no agreement among the rankings. Example 4.3 illustrates another situation where only the rankings of the variables are available from the research study.

Example 4.3

Rubenstein (1982) reports on a statistical analysis conducted to determine the current state of happiness and well-being of people living in different regions of the United States. The country was divided into nine nonoverlapping geographical regions. The data used to rank the regions were derived from studies conducted by the Institute for Social Research at the University of Michigan. Survey respondents answered 39 questions concerning quality of life. These questions covered six different aspects of well-being, labeled outlook on life, stress, positive feelings, negative feelings, personal competence, and overall satisfaction. For example, stress questions involved judgments of life as easy or hard, worries, fears, and so on. The real data rankings given by Rubenstein and shown in Table 4.8 for the nine regions on the six scales represent overall psychological well-being, with smaller numbers indicating greater well-being. For each scale, a 1 means best outlook on life, least stress, most positive feelings, least negative feelings, highest personal competence, and greatest overall satisfaction. Is there agreement among the rankings of the regions?

SOLUTION TO EXAMPLE 4.3:
KENDALL'S COEFFICIENT OF CONCORDANCE

We have $k = 6$ rankings of the $n = 9$ regions, where each ranking measures a different aspect of psychological well-being. We sum the ranks in each row of Table 4.8 to obtain the values 18, 19, 23, 24, 30, 30, 33, 45, and 48 for the respective regions. We find $S = 908$ from Equation 4.4, $W = .4204$ from Equation 4.3, and $Q = 20.18$ from Equation 4.6. As Q is distributed approximately as chi-square with 8 degrees of freedom, the P-value for the null hypothesis of no agreement among the rankings is $.001 < P < .01$ from Appendix Table E. We reject the null hypothesis and conclude that there is agreement among the

TABLE 4.8
Regional Ranks of Psychological Well-Being

Region	Outlook on Life	Stress	Positive Feelings	Negative Feelings	Personal Competence	Overall Satisfaction
West South Central	2	1	3	7	3	2
West North Central	7	2	4	1	2	3
New England	1	7	7	2	5	1
Mountain	6	6	1	4	1	6
Pacific	5	3	2	8	4	8
South Atlantic	4	4	5	5	7	5
East South Central	3	5	9	3	9	4
East North Central	9	8	6	9	6	7
Middle Atlantic	8	9	8	6	8	9

TABLE 4.9
Estimated Ranking of Regions

Rank	Region
1.5	West South Central
1.5	West North Central
3.0	New England
4.0	Mountain
5.5	Pacific
5.5	South Atlantic
7.0	East South Central
8.0	East North Central
9.0	Middle Atlantic

rankings of the regions; that is, the regions are similarly ranked high or low with respect to the six aspects of quality of life. In other words, if a region ranks high (low) on one aspect, there is a general tendency for that region to also rank high (low) on the other aspects of psychological well-being. The estimated preferential order of regions, based on the rank sums, is shown in Table 4.9.

The MINITAB and SPSSX package solutions to Example 4.3 are shown in Figures 4.7 and 4.8. Both results agree exactly with ours because we also used the chi-square approximation.

```
MTB > read aspect into c1, region into c2, ranks into c3
DATA>    1  1  2
DATA>    1  2  7
DATA>    1  3  1
DATA>    1  4  6
DATA>    1  5  5
DATA>    1  6  4
DATA>    1  7  3
DATA>    1  8  9
DATA>    1  9  8
DATA>    2  1  1
DATA>    2  2  2
DATA>    2  3  7
DATA>    2  4  6
DATA>    2  5  3
DATA>    2  6  4
DATA>    2  7  5
DATA>    2  8  8
DATA>    2  9  9
DATA>    3  1  3
DATA>    3  2  4
DATA>    3  3  7
DATA>    3  4  1
DATA>    3  5  2
DATA>    3  6  5
DATA>    3  7  9
DATA>    3  8  6
DATA>    3  9  8
DATA>    4  1  7
DATA>    4  2  1
DATA>    4  3  2
DATA>    4  4  4
DATA>    4  5  8
DATA>    4  6  5
DATA>    4  7  3
DATA>    4  8  9
DATA>    4  9  6
DATA>    5  1  3
DATA>    5  2  2
DATA>    5  3  5
DATA>    5  4  1
DATA>    5  5  4
DATA>    5  6  7
DATA>    5  7  9
```

continued

```
DATA>    5 8 6
DATA>    5 9 8
DATA>    6 1 2
DATA>    6 2 3
DATA>    6 3 1
DATA>    6 4 6
DATA>    6 5 8
DATA>    6 6 5
DATA>    6 7 4
DATA>    6 8 7
DATA>    6 9 9
       54 ROWS READ

MTB >   name c2='region'
MTB >   friedman c3 c2 c1

Friedman test of C3 by region blocked by C1

S = 20.18   d.f. = 8    p = 0.010
```

region	N	Est. Median	Sum of RANKS
W S C	6	2.722	18.0
W N C	6	2.889	19.0
N E	6	3.611	23.0
M O	6	4.278	24.0
P A	6	4.778	30.0
S A	6	4.889	30.0
E S C	6	4.833	33.0
E N C	6	7.389	45.0
M A	6	8.111	48.0

```
Grand median = 4.833
```

Figure 4.7. MINITAB Solution to Example 4.3

Kendall's coefficient of concordance is not a direct extension of Kendall's tau to more than two sets of rankings. Further, the value of Kendall's coefficient of concordance for $k = 2$ groups of n objects is not directly related to Kendall's tau. It is, however, related to Spearman's rho when $k = 2$ by the expression $W = (1 + r_s)/2$. Rho and tau always range between -1 and 1, whereas W always ranges between 0 and 1.

```
data list /wsc 1-2 wnc 3-4 ne 5-6 md 7-8 pa 9-10 sa 11-12
          esc 13-14 enc 15-16 ma 17-18
npar tests kendall=all
begin data
2 7 1 6 5 4 3 9 8
1 2 7 6 3 4 5 8 9
3 4 7 1 2 5 9 6 8
7 1 2 4 8 5 3 9 6
3 2 5 1 4 7 9 6 8
2 3 1 6 8 5 4 7 9
```

- - - - - Kendall Coefficient of concordance

Mean Rank	Variable
3.00	WSC
3.17	WNC
3.83	NE
4.00	MD
5.00	PA
5.00	SA
5.50	ESC
7.50	ENC
8.00	MA

Cases	W	Chi-Square	D.F.	Significance
6	.4204	20.1777	8	.0097

Figure 4.8. SPSSX Solution to Example 4.3

5. PARTIAL CORRELATION

Wallis and Roberts (1956, p. 79) give an example concerning a newspaper account that noted a positive correlation between the number of storks' nests and the number of human births in northwestern Europe. A reporter might speculate that this correlation gives evidence to support the myth that human babies are brought by storks. However, the real cause of this correlation was that population in general was growing in northwestern Europe, thereby increasing the number of buildings as places available for storks to nest. This is a case where the association between two variables is influenced by a third variable that was not taken into account for the analysis.

For this situation we need to calculate what is called a *coefficient of partial correlation*. Suppose there are three variables, X, Y, and Z, and we have a random sample of n triplets $(X_1, Y_1, Z_1), \ldots, (X_n, Y_n, Z_n)$. We want to measure the relationship between the variables X and Y when the effect of variable Z has been removed or partialed out. Kendall's *partial tau correlation coefficient* for X and Y when Z is held constant, or equivalently when the effect of Z has been removed, is calculated from

$$\tau_{XY.Z} = \frac{\tau_{XY} - \tau_{XZ}\tau_{YZ}}{\sqrt{1 - \tau_{XZ}^2}\sqrt{1 - \tau_{YZ}^2}}. \tag{5.1}$$

For substitution in Equation 5.1, τ_{XY} is calculated in the usual way from the pairs $(X_1, Y_1), \ldots, (X_n, Y_n)$, τ_{XZ} is calculated from the (X, Z) pairs, and τ_{YZ} is calculated from the (Y, Z) pairs, using Equation 2.3 if there are no ties. Midranks are used for ties, with each tau calculated from Equation 2.4.

The value of this partial tau correlation coefficient ranges between -1 and $+1$. If $\tau_{XY.Z} = 1$, X and Y are in complete agreement when Z is held constant in the following sense. Whenever an X pair is concordant with a Z pair, the corresponding Y pair is also concordant with that same Z pair, and whenever an X pair is discordant with a Z pair, the corresponding Y pair is also discordant with that same Z pair. In other words, X and Z are in perfect agreement and Y and Z are also in perfect agreement. If $\tau_{XY.Z} = -1$, X and Y are in complete disagreement when Z is held constant because whenever an X pair is concordant with a Z pair, the corresponding Y pair is discordant with that same Z pair, and vice versa. In other words, X is in perfect disagreement with Z, and Y is also in perfect disagreement with Z. If $\tau_{XY.Z} = 0$, the concordance between X and Z is independent of the concordance between Y and Z.

This interpretation of magnitudes of $\tau_{XY.Z}$ can be easily seen by expressing the formula in Equation 5.1 in a different way. We first make a table like Table 5.1 that shows the frequencies of pairwise concordances and discordances. The product ad is the number of times X and Y are both in perfect agreement with Z, and the product bc is the number of times X and Y are both in perfect disagreement with Z. It can be shown that the formula for $\tau_{XY.Z}$ in Equation 5.1 is equivalent to the formula

$$\tau_{XY.Z} = \frac{ad - bc}{\sqrt{(a + b)(c + d)(a + c)(b + d)}} \tag{5.2}$$

when there are no ties.

TABLE 5.1
Pairwise Concordances and Discordances

	Number of Y Pairs Concordant With Z Pairs	Number of Y Pairs Discordant With Z Pairs
Number of X pairs concordant with Z pairs	a	b
Number of X pairs discordant with Z pairs	c	d

Kendall's partial tau coefficient can be used to test the null hypothesis that the variables X and Y are independent when Z is held constant. Right-tail P-values for the sampling distribution of $\tau_{XY.Z}$ are given in Table F, Appendix A. The appropriate P-values are in the right tail of $\tau_{XY.Z}$ for the alternative of positive dependence, and in the right tail of $|\tau_{XY.Z}|$ for the alternative of negative dependence.

Example 5.1

The distraction hypothesis suggests that a message attempting to persuade persons to do something they do not want to do (discrepancy) will be more effective if the message is presented with distractions. This theory is attributed to Festinger and Maccoby (1964), who claim that distraction during exposure to discrepant information interferes with subvocal counterargumentation and thereby increases the audience's yielding to the persuasion attempt. Nelson, Duncan, and Frontczak (1985) investigated whether this concept applies to advertising. Subjects first completed a questionnaire designed to measure degree of discrepancy. Then subjects listened to radio commercial advertisements of a male home permanent product with distractions and later answered a questionnaire that provided information about level of distraction, involvement with the product, liking the commercial, liking the product, intention to buy the product, beliefs about the product, and counterargumentation (i.e., why the product would not be a good purchase). One of the hypotheses was that counterargumentation will show a negative relationship with distraction when message discrepancy is controlled. Test this hypothesis for the artificial data in Table 5.2 on 10 subjects.

TABLE 5.2
Subject Scores

Subject	Discrepancy	Distraction	Counterargu-mentation
1	1	7	0
2	3	15	1
3	7	25	2
4	4	26	3
5	5	20	4
6	6	19	4.1
7	8	22	4.5
8	8.5	17	5
9	8.8	10	7
10	9	27	8

SOLUTION TO EXAMPLE 5.1: PARTIAL TAU

We let X = distraction score, Y = counterargumentation score, and Z = discrepancy score, so that the test statistic to measure partial correlation is $\tau_{XY.Z}$. Table 5.3 lists the data with X in an ordered array and Table 5.4 shows Y in an ordered array, and the other columns show the respective calculations of C and D.

$$\tau_{XY} = \frac{2(26-19)}{10(9)} = .1556$$

$$\tau_{XZ} = \frac{2(27-18)}{10(9)} = .2000$$

$$\tau_{YZ} = \frac{2(42-3)}{10(9)} = .8667$$

$$\tau_{XY.Z} = \frac{.1556 - (.2000)(.8667)}{\sqrt{1-(.8667)^2}\,\sqrt{1-(.2000)^2}} = -.0364$$

There is a relatively strong positive correlation between counter-argumentation and discrepancy, Y and Z ($\tau_{YZ} = .8667$ and $P < .001$ from Table C, Appendix A), and this relationship between Y and Z has an effect on the relationship between distraction and counterargumentation,

TABLE 5.3
Calculations for (X, Y) and (X, Z)

X	Y	Z	X Rank	Y Rank	C	D	Z Rank	C	D
7	0	1	1	1	9	0	1	9	0
10	7	8.8	2	9	1	7	9	1	7
15	1	3	3	2	7	0	2	7	0
17	5	8.5	4	8	1	5	8	1	5
19	4.1	6	5	6	2	3	5	3	2
20	4	5	6	5	2	2	4	3	1
22	4.5	8	7	7	1	2	7	1	2
25	2	7	8	3	2	0	6	1	1
26	3	4	9	4	1	0	3	1	0
27	8	9	10	10			10		
					26	19		27	18

TABLE 5.4
Calculations for (Y, Z)

Y Rank	Z Rank	C	D
1	1	9	0
2	2	8	0
3	6	4	3
4	3	6	0
5	4	5	0
6	5	4	0
7	7	3	0
8	8	2	0
9	9	1	0
10	10		
		42	3

X and Y. The tau coefficient between X and Y is .1556 when Z is not taken into account, but the tau coefficient between X and Y when Z is taken into account is reduced to −.0364. This is a considerable reduction. However, neither of these values is significantly different from zero because $P > .05$ from Appendix Table E, in each case. This conclusion agrees with that found in Nelson et al. (1985).

The SAS solution to Example 5.1 (Figure 5.1) shows exactly the same pairwise values of Kendall's tau. The corresponding P-values given are

```
OPTIONS LINESIZE=80;
CMS FILEDEF RAWIN DISK EX5.1 DATA   K;
DATA A;
INFILE RAWIN;
INPUT SUBJ Z X Y;
LABEL Z = 'DISCREPANCY'
      X = 'DISTRACTION'
      Y = 'COUNTERARGUMENTATION';
PROC PRINT;
PROC CORR KENDALL;
VAR X Y;
PROC CORR KENDALL;
VAR X Z;
PROC CORR KENDALL;
VAR Y Z;
RUN;
```

```
                    OBS   SUBJ   Z    X    Y

                     1     1    1.0    7   0.0
                     2     2    3.0   15   1.0
                     3     3    7.0   25   2.0
                     4     4    4.0   26   3.0
                     5     5    5.0   20   4.0
                     6     6    6.0   19   4.1
                     7     7    8.0   22   4.5
                     8     8    8.5   17   5.0
                     9     9    8.8   10   7.0
                    10    10    9.0   27   8.0
```

Correlation Analysis

2 'VAR' Variables: X Y

Kendall Tau b Correlation Coefficients / Prob > |R| under Ho: Rho=0 / N = 10

	X	Y
X DISTRACTION	1.00000 0.0	0.15556 0.5312
Y COUNTERARGUMENTATION	0.15556 0.5312	1.00000 0.0

Correlation Analysis

2 'VAR' Variables: X Z

continued

Kendall Tau b Correlation Coefficients / Prob > |R| under Ho: Rho=0 / N = 10

	X	Z
X DISTRACTION	1.00000 0.0	0.20000 0.4208
Z DISCREPANCY	0.20000 0.4208	1.00000 0.0

Correlation Analysis

2 'VAR' Variables: Y   Z

Kendall Tau b Coefficients / Prob > |R| under Ho: Rho=0 / N = 10

	Y	Z
Y COUNTERARGUMENTATION	1.00000 0.0	0.86667 0.0005
Z DISCREPANCY	0.86667 0.0005	1.00000 0.0

Figure 5.1. SAS Solution to Example 5.1

two-tailed and are based on an approximation that is not very accurate for $n = 10$. Few if any computer packages include calculation of Kendall's partial tau. However, much of the calculation labor can be eliminated by using a package to calculate the ordinary tau between all possible pairs of data to obtain the results needed to substitute in Equation 5.1.

Because there are no ties in Example 5.1, we can also use these data to illustrate the calculation of $\tau_{XY.Z}$ from Equation 5.2. The first step is to list all possible X pairs, Y pairs, and Z pairs. There are $\binom{10}{2} = 45$ possible pairs of each in this case. The Z pairs are listed first in such a way that all Z pairs are concordant. This is shown in Table 5.5. The concordance is indicated by entering a plus sign (+) in the column labeled Z sign. Then each corresponding X pair is listed and noted in the X sign column as plus (+) for concordant or minus (−) for discordant; similarly for each corresponding Y pair. The value of a indicated in Table 5.1 is the total number of times the X sign and Y sign in Table 5.5 are both plus (+); here $a = 25$. The value of d is the total number of times

TABLE 5.5
Calculations for Equation 5.2

Z Pair	Z Sign	X Pair	X Sign	Y Pair	Y Sign
1,2	+	1,3	+	1,2	+
1,3	+	1,9	+	1,4	+
1,4	+	1,6	+	1,5	+
1,5	+	1,5	+	1,6	+
1,6	+	1,8	+	1,3	+
1,7	+	1,7	+	1,7	+
1,8	+	1,4	+	1,8	+
1,9	+	1,2	+	1,9	+
1,10	+	1,10	+	1,10	+
2,3	+	3,9	+	2,4	+
2,4	+	3,6	+	2,5	+
2,5	+	3,5	+	2,6	+
2,6	+	3,8	+	2,3	+
2,7	+	3,7	+	2,7	+
2,8	+	3,4	+	2,8	+
2,9	+	3,2	−	2,9	+
2,10	+	3,10	+	2,10	+
3,4	+	9,6	−	4,5	+
3,5	+	9,5	−	4,6	+
3,6	+	9,8	−	4,3	−
3,7	+	9,7	−	4,7	+
3,8	+	9,4	−	4,8	+
3,9	+	9,2	−	4,9	+
3,10	+	9,10	+	4,10	+
4,5	+	6,5	−	5,6	+
4,6	+	6,8	+	5,3	−
4,7	+	6,7	+	5,7	+
4,8	+	6,4	−	5,8	+
4,9	+	6,2	−	5,9	+
4,10	+	6,10	+	5,10	+
5,6	+	5,8	+	6,3	−
5,7	+	5,7	+	6,7	+
5,8	+	5,4	−	6,8	+
5,9	+	5,2	−	6,9	+
5,10	+	5,10	+	6,10	+
6,7	+	8,7	−	3,7	+
6,8	+	8,4	−	3,8	+
6,9	+	8,2	−	3,9	+
6,10	+	8,10	+	3,10	+
7,8	+	7,4	−	7,8	+
7,9	+	7,2	−	7,9	+
7,10	+	7,10	+	7,10	+
8,9	+	4,2	−	8,9	+
8,10	+	4,10	+	8,10	+
9,10	+	2,10	+	9,10	+

the X sign and Y sign are both minus (−), or $d = 1$. Similarly, b corresponds to X sign plus (+) and Y sign minus (−) or $b = 2$, and c corresponds to X sign minus (−) and Y sign plus (+) or $c = 17$. These values are substituted into Equation 5.2 to obtain

$$\tau_{XY.Z} = \frac{25 - 34}{\sqrt{27(18)(42)(3)}} = -.0364.$$

This agrees with the result calculated in Example 5.1 from Equation 5.1.

Example 5.2

Charlop and Carlson (1983) studied reversal shift learning in autistic children. A reversal shift involves teaching a child to respond to one stimulus of a stimulus pair and subsequently reversing the correct answer. For example, if a child is shown a "big" and "little" stimulus pair and taught that the correct answer is "big," the correct answer becomes "little" after a reversal shift. Previous research had indicated that ability to learn to make reversal shifts is related to chronological age for normal older children. Charlop and Carlson wanted to determine whether ability to make reversal shifts is still highly correlated with chronological age in a population where mental age is not so highly correlated with chronological age as with normal children. Therefore their study included only autistic children, in whom mental age and chronological age are not highly correlated. The study used nine autistic children with chronological ages (CA) between 2 and 14. Their mental ages (MA) were measured by a standardized test; the results ranged between 1.1 and 7.1. Ability to make reversal shifts (RS) was measured in this experiment by the number of trials required to learn the reversal shift. For the simulated data shown in Table 5.6, determine Kendall's partial tau coefficient between chronological age and ability to make reversal shifts when mental age is held constant. Because larger numbers of trials required to learn RS indicate lower performance, we would expect a negative association.

SOLUTION TO EXAMPLE 5.2: PARTIAL TAU

Let $X = $ CA, $Y = $ RS, and $Z = $ MA, so that we are looking for $\tau_{XY.Z}$. We rank each set of scores from 1 to 9 and reorder the scores so that X is in an ordered array in Table 5.7, and Z is in an ordered array in Table 5.8.

TABLE 5.6

Children's Scores

Child	CA	MA	RS
1	13.3	6.0	10
2	6.5	3.7	72
3	11.2	2.1	27
4	13.1	1.1	29
5	10.2	5.9	10
6	11.1	6.5	11
7	11.6	4.3	15
8	9.3	4.9	25
9	9.7	7.1	10

TABLE 5.7

Scores With X in an Ordered Array

Child	X	Z	C	D	Y	C	D
1	1	3	6	2	9	0	8
8	2	5	4	3	6	2	5
9	3	9	0	6	2	4	0
5	4	6	2	3	2	4	0
6	5	8	0	4	4	3	1
3	6	2	2	1	7	1	2
7	7	4	1	1	5	1	1
4	8	1	1	0	8	0	1
1	9	7	16	20	2	15	18

TABLE 5.8

Scores With Z in an Ordered Array

Child	Z	Y	C	D
4	1	8	1	7
3	2	7	1	6
2	3	9	0	6
7	4	5	1	4
8	5	6	0	4
5	6	2	1	0
1	7	2	1	0
6	8	4	0	1
9	9	2	5	28

```
OPTIONS LINESIZE=80;
CMS FILEDEF RAWIN DISK EX5.2 DATA     K;
DATA A;
INFILE RAWIN;
INPUT CHILD    X Y Z;
LABEL X = 'CA'
      Y = 'RS'
      Z = 'MA';
PROC PRINT;
PROC CORR KENDALL;
 VAR X Y;
PROC CORR KENDALL;
 VAR X Z;
PROC CORR KENDALL;
 VAR Y Z;
RUN;
```

OBS	CHILD	X	Z	Y
1	1	13.3	6.0	10
2	2	6.5	3.7	72
3	3	11.2	2.1	27
4	4	13.1	1.1	29
5	5	10.2	5.9	10
6	6	11.1	6.5	11
7	7	11.6	4.3	15
8	8	9.3	4.9	25
9	9	9.7	7.1	10

Correlation Analysis

2 'VAR' Variables: X   Z

Kendall Tau b Correlation Coefficients / Prob > |R| under Ho: Rho=0 / N = 9

	X	Z
X	1.00000	−0.11111
CA	0.0	0.6767
Z	−0.11111	1.00000
MA	0.6767	0.0

Correlation Analysis

2 'VAR' Variables: X   Y

continued

Kendall Tau b Correlation Coefficients / Prob > |R| under Ho: Rho=0 / N = 9

	X	Y
X	1.00000	-0.08704
CA	0.0	0.7496
Y	-0.08704	1.00000
RS	0.7496	0.0

Correlation Analysis

2 'VAR' Variables: Z   Y

Kendall Tau b Correlation Coefficients / Prob > |R| under Ho: Rho=0 / N = 9

	Z	Y
Z	1.00000	-0.66730
MA	0.0	0.0144
Y	-0.66730	1.00000
RS	0.0144	0.0

Figure 5.2. SAS Solution to Example 5.2

There are ties in the Y scores, so we have to be very careful in calculating C and D for those pairs involving Y. Using Equation 2.4 for tau$_b$, we find $\tau_{XZ} = -.1111$, $\tau_{XY} = -.0870$, $\tau_{YZ} = -.6673$. We substitute these tau$_b$ values in Equation 5.1 to obtain $\tau_{XY.Z} = -.2178$. We refer $\tau_{XY.Z}$ to Appendix Table F and τ_{XY} to Table C. Both have P-values greater than .05, and so we cannot conclude that either is significantly negative. We do note, however, that the absolute value of $\tau_{XY.Z}$ is almost three times as large as that of τ_{XY}, so that Z seems to be associated with both X and Y to some extent, but more with Y than with X.

The SAS printout depicted in Figure 5.2 shows these calculations of pairwise τ_b values for Example 5.2, which agree with ours. The P-values given for all pairs are two-tailed and are based on an approximation that will not be very accurate with $n = 9$.

The parametric measure of partial correlation for three variables that corresponds to Kendall's partial tau in Equation 5.1 is the Pearson partial correlation coefficient computed from

60

$$r_{XY.Z} = \frac{r_{XY} - r_{XZ} r_{YZ}}{\sqrt{1 - r_{XZ}^2}\sqrt{1 - r_{YZ}^2}}, \qquad (5.3)$$

where r_{XY}, r_{XZ}, and r_{YZ} are the Pearson product-moment correlation coefficients. A different nonparametric partial correlation coefficient can be obtained by substituting the Spearman rank correlation coefficients for r_{XY}, r_{XZ}, and r_{YZ} in Equation 5.3. However, tables of the exact sampling distribution of such a coefficient are not generally available. The concept of partial correlation can easily be extended to more than three variables. For example, with four variables, X_1, X_2, X_3, and X_4, the basic parametric formula is

$$r_{12.34} = \frac{r_{12.3} - r_{13.4} r_{23.4}}{\sqrt{1 - r_{13.4}^2}\sqrt{1 - r_{23.4}^2}}. \qquad (5.4)$$

Thus when X_4 is also taken into account, the partial correlation is a function of the individual partial correlation coefficients involving three variables. Either Kendall's tau or Spearman's rho can be substituted into Equation 5.4 to obtain a nonparametric partial correlation coefficient for four variables. Tables of the sampling distribution are not generally available, however.

6. MEASURES OF ASSOCIATION IN ORDERED CONTINGENCY TABLES

A two-way contingency table is a joint classification of a group of subjects according to two or more levels of two primary variables or factors, which we call A and B. For example, the primary variables might be highest level of formal education completed (A) and socioeconomic status 20 years after completing education (B). The levels of education might be less than 12 years (A_1), high school graduate (A_2), some college (A_3), college graduate (A_4), and postgraduate (A_5). The levels of socioeconomic status might be levels of income or occupational status. Each subject in the sample is classified into exactly one level of each of the two primary variables, and the frequencies of cross-classification are presented in a two-way table such as the one shown in Table 6.1. This kind of table is called a contingency table.

TABLE 6.1
A Generic Contingency Table

Primary Variable A	B_1	B_2	$\ldots$	B_c	Row Totals
		Primary Variable B			
A_1	f_{11}	f_{12}	$\ldots$	f_{1c}	$f_{1.}$
A_2	f_{21}	f_{22}	$\ldots$	f_{2c}	$f_{2.}$
.	.	.	$\ldots$	.	.
.	.	.	$\ldots$	.	.
.	.	.	$\ldots$	.	.
A_r	f_{r1}	f_{r2}	$\ldots$	f_{rc}	$f_{r.}$
Column totals	$f_{.1}$	$f_{.2}$		$f_{.c}$	n

The table has r rows and c columns when there are r levels of variable A and c levels of variable B. The notation is that f_{ij} is the number of subjects that were classified as being in both of the levels A_i and B_j. The row total $f_{i.}$ indicates the number of subjects classified in level A_i, irrespective of the B-level classification. The column total $f_{.j}$ represents the number of subjects in level B_j, irrespective of the A-level classification.

The most common method of significance testing for data cast in a contingency table is called the chi-square test of independence. It is appropriate for the null hypothesis of independence between the variables A and B against the alternative that A and B are not independent or have some kind of association. The chi-square test is sensitive to nonindependence of all kinds, not just association or association in a particular direction. Further, this test statistic is only approximately distributed as chi-square regardless of the sample size. The exact sampling distribution of the so-called chi-square test statistic is not known. The value of the test statistic is highly inflated by small expected frequencies, and the test almost always leads to rejection of the null hypothesis if the sample size is large. The chi-square test does not allow us to have a one-sided alternative stating that association exists in a particular direction. Several different descriptive measures of association are based on the value of the chi-square statistic, but they cannot be interpreted easily in general.

If the variables A and B are each measured on at least an ordinal scale (as opposed to nominal labels), the levels will also be ordinal and the chi-square test of independence is not appropriate. This is also true when the variables are qualitative (with nominal labels) but the levels are ordinal. In each case, interchanging two rows or two columns of the contingency table would not change the value of the chi-square test statistic but would completely alter any ordered relationships in the original data. Further, in such a case, when we reject the null hypothesis of no association we generally will not be content with the conclusion of dependence or that association exists. We want to know a direction for the association. Ordinal variables and/or ordinal levels in a contingency table call for tests that make use of these order relationships and allow us to determine the direction of association between variables. The association is positive if an increase in the level of one variable usually occurs in conjunction with an increase in the level of the other variable. The association is negative if an increase in the level of one variable tends to occur with a decrease in the level of the other variable.

This chapter covers in detail two tests that take into account the order relationships expressed by the levels of the variables. These two procedures are based on Spearman's rho and Kendall's tau coefficients. Three related measures of ordinal association, called tau_c, the Goodman and Kruskal gamma coefficient, and Somers's d, will also be discussed briefly. Each of these methods is easier to explain by a numerical example than in general. The entire test procedure based on Spearman's rho will be shown in detail in Example 6.1, and the process based on Kendall's tau will be shown in Examples 6.2 and 6.3.

Example 6.1

Suppose that 100 subjects were asked to respond on a 3-point Likert scale regarding their attitudes toward the importance of formal education and the importance of socioeconomic status, producing the hypothetical data shown in Table 6.2. The variables attitude toward education and attitude toward status are nominal labels but the levels are ordinal in each case. We would like to test the null hypothesis that attitudes toward education and status are independent or have no association against the alternative that attitudes toward education and status are positively associated. A chi-square test would not be useful for this purpose.

On the Likert scale we let 1 = very important and 3 = little importance. The 30 subjects who responded "very important" to Education cannot be rank ordered and are essentially tied; each one would be given the education midrank $(1 + 2 + \ldots + 30)/30 = 15.5$, or equivalently $(1 + 30)/2 = 15.5$. The 50 subjects who responded "indifferent" to

TABLE 6.2

Responses of Subjects

Attitude Toward Status	Attitude Toward Education			Total
	Very Important	Indifferent	Little Importance	
Very Important	20	10	6	36
Indifferent	5	30	4	39
Little Importance	5	10	10	25
Total	30	50	20	100

Education are tied for education ranks 31, 32, . . . , 80. Hence the education midrank for this group is $(31 + 80)/2 = 40.5$. The 20 subjects regarding education to be of little importance are tied for education ranks 81, 82, . . . , 100 and their midrank is $(81 + 100)/2 = 90.5$. The 36 subjects who responded "very important" to status are all given the status midrank $(1 + 36)/2 = 18.5$. In this manner we can obtain 100 pairs of ranks and compute either Spearman's rho or Kendall's tau to measure the association between the two sets of attitudes. Such a calculation is tedious and there is a much easier way, as will be shown in the solutions to the examples in this chapter.

SOLUTION TO EXAMPLE 6.1: SPEARMAN'S RHO

Table 6.3 shows the quantities needed to calculate rho, using midranks for all of the ties. Because there are 20 pairs of subjects tied for education rank 1 (these subjects have midrank 15.5) and status rank 1 (which have midrank 18.5), their contribution to Σd^2 is $20(15.5 - 18.5)^2$ $= 180$. We continue in this manner to obtain the total $\Sigma d^2 = 94{,}810$. This result will be substituted into Equation 2.2, but we also need to calculate the corrections for ties, as shown in Table 6.4.

Finally, we substitute these results in Equation 2.2 to obtain

$$r_s = \frac{100^3 - 100 - 6(94{,}810) - 6(10{,}125 + 13{,}325)}{\sqrt{100^3 - 100 - 121{,}500}\,\sqrt{100^3 - 100 - 159{,}900}} = .3380.$$

To test the null hypothesis of independence, we can calculate the standard normal test statistic from Equation 3.1 as $Z = .3380\sqrt{99} = 3.36$. The result is significant ($P = .0004$ from Table A, Appendix A), and we conclude that there exists a significant positive association between

TABLE 6.3
Calculation of Rho

Education Attitude	Status Attitude	Frequency	Education Midrank	Status Midrank	Contribution to Σd^2
1	1	20	15.5	18.5	180
1	2	5	15.5	56	8,201.25
1	3	5	15.5	88	26,281.25
2	1	10	55.5	18.5	13,690
2	2	30	55.5	56	7.50
2	3	10	55.5	88	10,562.50
3	1	6	90.5	18.5	31,104
3	2	4	90.5	56	4,761
3	3	10	90.5	88	22.5
					94,810

TABLE 6.4
Calculation of Ties Corrections

t	t^3	u	u^3
36	46,656	30	27,000
39	59,319	50	125,000
25	15,625	20	8,000
100	121,600	100	160,000

$$t' = \frac{121,600 - 100}{12} = 10,125 \qquad u' = \frac{160,000 - 100}{12} = 13,325$$

attitude toward education and attitude toward socioeconomic status. In other words, people who regard education as very important also tend to regard socioeconomic status as very important.

The SAS solution to Example 6.1, shown in Figure 6.1, agrees with ours except for rounding. It incorporates the correction for ties.

Example 6.2

Stevenson (1990) proposed models to explain networks of work-related social interaction of persons within organizations in relation to

```
OPTIONS LINESIZE=80;
CMS FILEDEF RAWIN DISK EX61   DATA    A1  ;
DATA A;
INFILD RAWIN;
INPUT A B FREQ ;
  LABEL A = 'ATTITUDE TOWARD STATUS'
        B = 'ATTITUDE TOWARD EDUCATION';
PROC PRINT;
PROC CORR SPEARMAN;
  VAR A B;
  FREQ  FREQ ;
RUN;
```

OBS	A	B	FREQ
1	1	1	20
2	1	2	10
3	1	3	6
4	2	1	5
5	2	2	30
6	2	3	4
7	3	1	5
8	3	2	10
9	3	3	10

SPEARMAN CORRELATION COEFFICIENTS
/ PROB > |R| UNDER HO:RHO=0 / N = 100 / FREQ VAR=FREQ

	A	B
A	1.00000	0.33772
ATTITUDE TOWARD STATUS	0.0000	0.0006
B	0.33772	1.00000
ATTITUDE TOWARD EDUCATION	0.0006	0.0000

Figure 6.1. SAS Solution to Example 6.1

the hierarchical organizational structure. Data were collected from all managerial and professional employees of a West Coast public transit agency. One part of the questionnaire asked employees to list those managerial and professional employees with whom they interacted in order to get the job done; this information enabled the researcher to test the null hypothesis of no association in the social interaction between the hierarchical level in the organization of the initiator and recipient

TABLE 6.5
Linkages Among Hierarchical Levels

| Initiator of Communication | Recipient of Communication | | | |
	Top	Middle	Bottom	Total
Top	159	55	24	238
Middle	123	94	136	353
Bottom	141	215	300	656
Total	423	364	460	1,247

of work-related communications. All employees participating were classified into one of three vertical hierarchical levels, called Top, Middle, and Bottom. Top Level included directors, department heads, and staff reporting directly to them; Middle Level included division heads; Bottom Level included all other professionals. The real data in Table 6.5 show the classification of communication linkages between individuals at the three levels as determined from the work interaction answers to the questionnaire. For example, 159 participants at the Top Level sent communications to other Top Level employees in order to get the job done. The asymmetry of numbers in this table suggests that there will be association, and specifically that the Top and Bottom Level persons tend to interact mostly within their own hierarchical level, whereas Middle Level persons act as intermediaries or buffers between those in the other two levels. Analyze the data to see if there is a positive association between levels of initiator and recipient.

SOLUTION TO EXAMPLE 6.2: KENDALL'S TAU

We give rank 1 to Top Level in each case and rank 3 to Bottom Level. The upper left-hand cell of Table 6.5 represents the pairs of observations that are all tied at $(1,1)$. Letting the first member of each pair denote the rank indicated by the row, we have the (i,j) frequency representing persons with initiator rank i and recipient rank j. The pairs concordant with the 159 $(1,1)$ pairs are all those with ranks $(2,2)$, $(2,3)$, $(3,2)$, and $(3,3)$, which total $159(94 + 136 + 215 + 300) = 118,455$ concordant pairs. No pairs are discordant with these $(1,1)$ pairs. The pairs concordant with the 55 $(1,2)$ pairs are those with ranks $(2,3)$ and $(3,3)$, which total $55(136 + 300) = 23,980$. The pairs discordant with the 55 $(1,2)$ pairs are those with ranks $(2,1)$ and $(3,1)$, which total

TABLE 6.6
Calculation of C and D

Pair	C			D		
(1,1)	159(94 + 136 + 215 + 300)	=	118,455	159(0)	=	0
(1,2)	55(136 + 300)	=	23,980	55(123 + 141)	=	14,520
(1,3)	24(0)	=	0	24(123+141+94+215)	=	13,752
(2,1)	123(215 + 300)	=	63,345	123(0)	=	0
(2,2)	94(300)	=	28,200	94(141)	=	13,254
(2,3)	136(0)	=	0	136(141 + 215)	=	48,416
(3,1)	141(0)	=	0	141(0)	=	0
(3,2)	215(0)	=	0	215(0)	=	0
(3,3)	300(0)	=	0	300(0)	=	0
			233,980			89,942

TABLE 6.7
Calculation of Corrections for Ties

t	$(t^2 - t)/2$	u	$(u^2 - u)/2$
238	28,203	423	89,253
353	62,128	364	66,066
656	214,840	460	105,570
	305,171		260,889

$55(123 + 141) = 14,520$. We continue counting in this way as shown in Table 6.6 to find the total numbers of concordant and discordant pairs.

Because the ties are quite extensive, we now need to calculate the corrections for ties in Equation 2.4 for tau_b. Each row and column in Table 6.5 contains some kind of tie between pairs. The row totals represent ties in the Initiator variable and the column totals represent ties in the Recipient variable. The necessary calculations are shown in Table 6.7. The total number of pairs is $1,247(1,246)/2 = 776,881$, and substitution in Equation 2.4 gives

$$\tau_b = \frac{233,980 - 89,942}{\sqrt{776,881 - 305,171}\sqrt{776,881 - 260,889}} = .2920.$$

The sample size is very large here, as it usually is with contingency tables, and so the test will be based on the normal approximation to the distribution of τ_b. However, when the ties are as extensive as they are here the variance of τ_b given in the normal approximation statistic in Equation 3.2 also needs to be corrected for ties. We give the formula for Z in terms of $S = C - D$, the difference between the numbers of concordant and discordant pairs, because the calculations are simpler. The formula is

$$Z = \frac{S \pm 1}{\sqrt{\text{Var}(S)}}, \qquad (6.1)$$

where the 1 in the numerator is a correction for continuity; the plus is used if S is negative and the minus is used if S is positive. The variance of S in the denominator of Equation 6.1 can be calculated from the expression

$$\text{Var}(S) = \frac{n(n-1)(2n+5)}{18} \qquad (6.2)$$

$$- \frac{1}{18}\left[\sum(t^2 - t)(2t + 5) + \sum(u^2 - u)(2u + 5)\right]$$

$$+ \frac{1}{9n(n-1)(n-2)}\left[\sum(t^2 - t)(t - 2)\right]\left[\sum(u^2 - u)(u - 2)\right]$$

$$+ \frac{1}{2n(n-1)}\left[\sum(t^2 - t)\right]\left[\sum(u^2 - u)\right].$$

Table 6.8 shows these calculations for our example.

The variance of S from Equation 6.2 is then

$$\text{Var}(S) = \frac{1,247(1,246)(2,499)}{18} - \frac{(681,365,862 + 444,065,862)}{18}$$

$$+ \frac{(337,936,392)(219,684,930)}{9(1,247)(1,246)(1,245)} + \frac{(610,342)(521,778)}{2(1,247)(1,246)}$$

$$= 157,556,667.1$$

and our test statistic from Equation 6.1 is $Z = 11.48$. The approximate P-value from Table A is less than .0002, so we conclude that there is a

TABLE 6.8
Calculations for Var(S)

t	$(t^2 - t)(2t + 5)$	$(t^2 - t)(t - 2)$	u	$(u^3 - u)(2u + 5)$	$(u^2 - u)(u - 2)$
238	27,131,286	13,311,816	423	151,908,606	75,151,026
353	88,346,016	43,613,856	364	96,852,756	47,831,784
656	565,888,560	281,010,720	460	195,304,500	96,702,120
	681,365,862	337,936,392		444,065,862	219,684,930

significant positive relationship. Even though the absolute magnitude of τ_b is small, it is large relative to its standard deviation and this produces a large value of Z and confirms a significant relationship.

The SAS and SPSSX solutions to Example 6.2 are shown in Figures 6.2 and 6.3. The SAS solution calculates tau_b with the correction for ties and an approximate standard error (labeled ASE) but no P-value. The SPSSX solution gives the same value for tau_b and also one form of the approximate standard error (labeled ASE1) and the value of an approximate T test statistic that is similar to our approximate Z test statistic. No P-value is given.

With data in an ordered contingency table, the Stuart-Kendall coefficient τ_c is sometimes used instead of τ_b because $|\tau_b| < 1$ if $r \neq c$. The formula is

$$\tau_c = \frac{2m(C - D)}{n^2(m - 1)}, \tag{6.3}$$

where $m = \min(r,c)$. This formula has a correction for the dimensions of the contingency table but no correction for ties. Hence it is more closely akin to τ_a (based on Equation 2.3) than to τ_b. In Example 6.2, $m = 3$ and the calculation from Equation 6.3 is

$$\tau_c = \frac{2(3)(233,980 - 89,942)}{1,247^2(2)} = .2779.$$

The absolute value of τ_c is smaller than $|\tau_b|$, as it always will be as long as $n \geq m$. The SAS and SPSSX solutions to Example 6.2 also show this result.

A different but related measure of association that can be calculated for data in an ordered contingency table is the Goodman-Kruskal gamma coefficient defined by

```
OPTIONS LINESIZE=80;
CMS FILEDEF RAWIN DISK EX6.2 DATA    A1  ;
DATA A;
INFILE RAWIN;
INPUT A B FREQ ;
  LABEL A = 'INITIATOR OF COMMUNICATION'
        B = 'RECIPIENT OF COMMUNICATION';
PROC FREQ DATA=A;
 TABLES A*B / MEASURES;
 WEIGHT FREQ;
RUN;
```

```
TABLE OF A BY B

A(INITIATOR OF COMMUNICATION)    B(RECIPIENT OF COMMUNICATION)
FREQUENCY |
 PERCENT  |
 ROW PCT  |
 COL PCT  |        1 |       2 |       3 |  TOTAL
- - - - - |- - - - -|- - - - -|- - - - -|
        1 |    159  |    55   |    24   |   238
          |  12.75  |  4.41   |  1.92   |  19.09
          |  66.81  | 23.11   | 10.08   |
          |  37.59  | 15.11   |  5.22   |
- - - - - |- - - - -|- - - - -|- - - - -|-
        2 |    123  |    94   |   136   |   353
          |   9.86  |  7.54   | 10.91   |  28.31
          |  34.84  | 26.63   | 38.53   |
          |  29.08  | 25.82   | 29.57   |
- - - - - |- - - - -|- - - - -|- - - - -|-
        3 |    141  |   215   |   300   |   656
          |  11.31  | 17.24   | 24.06   |  52.61
          |  21.49  | 32.77   | 45.73   |
          |  33.33  | 59.07   | 65.22   |
- - - - - |- - - - -|- - - - -|- - - - -|
TOTAL          423       364       460      1247
             33.92     29.19     36.89    100.00
```

continued

$$\gamma = \frac{C - D}{C + D}.$$ (6.4)

Like τ_b, the value of this coefficient ranges between -1 and 1 with the same interpretation of magnitude. The primary difference is that γ can actually achieve the values -1 and $+1$, whereas the largest possible

71

STATISTICS FOR TABLE OF A BY B

STATISTIC	VALUE	ASE
GAMMA	0.445	0.033
KENDALL'S TAU-B	0.292	0.023
STUART'S TAU-C	0.278	0.023
SOMERS' D C|R	0.305	0.024
SOMERS' D R|C	0.279	0.023
PEARSON CORRELATION	0.345	0.025
SPEARMAN CORRELATION	0.327	0.026
LAMBDA ASYMMETRIC C|R	0.172	0.016
LAMBDA ASYMMETRIC R|C	0.030	0.029
LAMBDA SYMMETRIC	0.111	0.020
UNCERTAINTY COEFFICIENT C|R	0.066	0.009
UNCERTAINTY COEFFICIENT R|C	0.071	0.010
UNCERTAINTY COEFFICIENT SYM	0.068	0.010

SAMPLE SIZE = 1247

ASE IS THE ASYMPTOTIC STANDARD ERROR.
R|C MEANS ROW VARIABLE DEPENDENT ON COLUMN VARIABLE.

Figure 6.2. SAS Solution to Example 6.2

value for $|\tau_b|$ may be smaller than 1. This is true because the denominator of γ, $C + D$, is equal to the exact number of pairs (X_i, Y_i), (X_j, Y_j) that are either concordant or discordant, that is, the number of pairs that are not tied. The denominator of τ_b incorporates a correction for ties that provides an estimate of $C + D$, the number of untied pairs. Thus the only difference between γ and τ_b is the method of correction for ties. In Example 6.2, the Goodman-Kruskal γ coefficient from Equation 6.4 is

$$\gamma = (233,980 - 89,942)/(233,980 + 89,942) = .4447.$$

The absolute value of this result is larger than τ_b, as is always the case. The SAS and SPSSX solutions to Example 6.2 also show this result. Tests of significance for γ require special tables (see Goodman & Kruskal, 1963, 1972, 1980).

72

```
data list        /freq 1-5 a 7 b 9
weight by        freq
crosstabs        tables= a by b
options          3,5
STATISTICS       6,7,8,9
begin data
159     1 1
55      1 2
24      1 3
123     2 1
94      2 2
136     2 3
141     3 1
215     3 2
300     3 3
end data
```

A BY B

```
  Count  |
  Row Pct|           B
  Tot Pct|                              Row
         |    1   |    2 |    3   | Total
  - - - -|- - -|- - -|- - - -|
     1   |  159  |  55  |   24   |  238
         | 66.8  | 23.1 |  10.1  |  19.1
         | 12.8  |  4.4 |   1.9  |
  - - - -|- - -|- - -|- - - -+
     2   |  123  |  94  |  136   |  353
  A      | 34.8  | 26.6 |  38.5  |  28.3
         |  9.9  |  7.5 |  10.9  |
  - - - -|- - - -|- - -|- - - -|
     3   |  141  |  215 |  300   |  656
         | 21.5  | 32.8 |  45.7  |  52.6
         | 11.3  | 17.2 |  24.1  |
  - - - -|- - -|- - -|- - - -+
  Column   423     364    460     1247
  Total   33.9    29.2   36.9    100.0
```

	Value	ASE1	T-value	Approximate Significance
Statistic				
Kendall's Tau-b	.29196	.02340	12.26816	
Kendall's Tau-c	.27789	.02265	12.26816	
Gamma	.44467	.03327	12.26816	
Somers' D :				
symmetric	.29166	.02338	12.26816	
with A dependent	.27915	.02281	12.26816	
with B dependent	.30535	.02418	12.26816	

Figure 6.3. SPSSX Solution to Example 6.2

Another related measure of association for ordered contingency tables is called Somers's d. This measure is appropriate when one of the primary variables is designated as an independent variable and the other is the dependent variable. The formula when A is the independent variable is

$$d_{B.A} = \frac{2(C - D)}{n^2 - \sum\limits_{i=1}^{r} f_{i.}^2}, \quad (6.5)$$

and when B is the independent variable, we have

$$d_{A.B} = \frac{2(C - D)}{n^2 - \sum\limits_{j=1}^{c} f_{.j}^2}. \quad (6.6)$$

Note that the denominator in $d_{B.A}$ corrects for the ties in the levels of A, and $d_{A.B}$ corrects for ties in B. The product of these two measures is equal to the square of Kendall's tau$_b$ or, equivalently, τ_b is equal to the geometric mean of Equations 6.5 and 6.6. The values of $d_{B.A}$ and $d_{A.B}$ always range between -1 and 1, with the same interpretation as for τ_b. In Example 6.2,

$$d_{B.A} = \frac{2(233,980 - 89,942)}{1,247^2 - 238^2 - 353^2 - 656^2} = .3054,$$

$$d_{A.B} = \frac{2(333,980 - 89,942)}{1,247^2 - 423^2 - 364^2 - 460^2} = .2791,$$

and the product $d_{B.A} d_{A.B} = .085 = \tau_b^2$. The SAS and SPSSX solutions to Example 6.2 show these results.

Because the exact standard error of each of these test statistics for testing no association in ordered contingency tables is dependent upon the null distribution of the population and on the configuration of ties, several different expressions have been developed to obtain an approximate standard error. Most of the formulas are quite complicated. Somers (1980) came up with some approximation formulas for the standard errors of τ_b, γ, and Somers's d that are quite simple to calculate because they are functions of only r and c, the dimensions of the contingency table. These approximations are based on the assumption of multinomial sampling from a uniform distribution, but Somers found them to be quite accurate for other distributions also; thus they are included in this volume.

The approximate standard error of τ_b is $\sqrt{4(r+1)(c+1)/9nrc}$, and hence the approximate standard normal test statistic to use in place of Equation 6.1 is

$$Z = \frac{3\tau_b\sqrt{nrc}}{2\sqrt{(r+1)(c+1)}} . \tag{6.7}$$

For the Goodman and Kruskal gamma coefficient the approximate standard error is $\sqrt{4(r+1)(c+1)/9n(r-1)(c-1)}$ and thus the approximate normal test statistic is

$$Z = \frac{3\gamma\sqrt{n(r-1)(c-1)}}{2\sqrt{(r+1)(c+1)}} . \tag{6.8}$$

For Somers's $d_{A.B}$ the approximate standard error is

$$\sqrt{4(r^2-1)(c+1)/9nr^2(c-1)}$$

and the approximate normal test statistic is

$$Z = \frac{3d_{A.B}\sqrt{nr^2(c-1)}}{2\sqrt{(r^2-1)(c+1)}} . \tag{6.9}$$

For Example 6.2, we have $r = c = 3$ and $n = 1,247$. The calculations from Equations 6.7, 6.8, and 6.9 for the approximate normal test statistics for τ_b, γ, and $d_{A.B}$ are, respectively,

$$Z = \frac{3(.2920)\sqrt{1,247(3)(3)}}{2\sqrt{4(4)}} = 11.60,$$

$$Z = \frac{3(.4447)\sqrt{1,247(2)(2)}}{2\sqrt{4(4)}} = 11.78,$$

and

$$Z = \frac{3(.2791)\sqrt{1,247(3)^2(2)}}{2\sqrt{(3^2 - 1)(4)}} = 11.09 .$$

For each statistic, Appendix Table A shows that $P < .0002$, and we conclude that the variables have a positive association.

In the special case where an ordered contingency table has $r = 2$ rows and $c = 2$ columns, S can be calculated as $S = f_{11}f_{22} - f_{12}f_{21}$, and Kendall's τ_b with the correction for ties in Equation 2.4 can be more easily calculated from the expression

$$\tau_b = \frac{f_{11}f_{22} - f_{12}f_{21}}{\sqrt{f_{1.}f_{2.}f_{.1}f_{.2}}} . \qquad (6.10)$$

This formula says that in the 2×2 table, take the product of the frequencies on the main diagonal minus the product of the frequencies on the off-diagonal and divide by the square root of the product of all row and column sums. The corresponding tau_c coefficient from Equation 6.3 for 2×2 tables is

$$\tau_c = \frac{4(f_{11}f_{22} - f_{12}f_{21})}{n^2} \qquad (6.11)$$

and the corresponding Goodman-Kruskal coefficient from Equation 6.4 for 2×2 tables can be calculated as

$$\gamma = \frac{f_{11}f_{22} - f_{12}f_{21}}{f_{11}f_{22} + f_{12}f_{21}} . \qquad (6.12)$$

This gamma for 2×2 tables is sometimes referred to as Yule's Q.

The corresponding Somers's d coefficients from Equations 6.5 and 6.6 for 2×2 tables can be expressed as

$$d_{B.A} = \frac{2(f_{11}f_{22} - f_{12}f_{21})}{n^2 - f_{1.}^2 - f_{2.}^2} \qquad (6.13)$$

and

76

TABLE 6.9
Number of "Don't Know" Responses

	No Prior Debriefing	Prior Debriefing	Total
Unbiased instruction	68	52	120
Biased Instruction	103	42	145
Total	171	94	265

$$d_{A.B} = \frac{2(f_{11}f_{22} - f_{12}f_{21})}{n^2 - f_{.1}^2 - f_{.2}^2}. \tag{6.14}$$

The next example illustrates these calculations for data in a 2×2 table.

Example 6.3

Kohnken and Maass (1985) investigated the effects of biased instructions on the accuracy of identification among suspects by eyewitnesses to a crime. The subjects were college students and the theft of a bag was staged during a lecture in three classrooms. One week later, subjects were asked by the police to identify the thief from a lineup of seven similar-looking persons, excluding the thief. The identification process allowed each subject to identify exactly one member of the lineup as the thief, or to say that the thief was not among the lineup persons, or to say that he or she did not know. Some of the subjects were "debriefed" just before the identification process; this debriefing told the subjects that an experiment was being carried out and the results of the experiment were of great importance for future criminal investigations and court trials. Some of the subjects were given biased instructions that clearly implied that the police thought the perpetrator was among the seven persons in the lineup, but that the subject should be absolutely certain of the identification. One of the research hypotheses was that subjects receiving no prior debriefing and biased instructions would give a greater number of "don't know" identifications than subjects in any other condition. The data given in Table 6.9 on number of "don't know" identifications for 265 subjects are artificial, but the relative magnitudes are comparable to those reported in the study.

SOLUTION TO EXAMPLE 6.3: KENDALL'S TAU

We will call Instruction the A variable and Debriefing the B variable, and assign rank 1 to each of No Prior Debriefing and Unbiased Instruction and rank 2 to each of Prior Debriefing and Biased Instruction. The null hypothesis is independence between Debriefing Type and Instruction Form and the research hypothesis calls for an alternative of negative association. The test statistic from Equation 6.10 is

$$\tau_b = \frac{68(42) - 52(103)}{\sqrt{171(94)(120)(145)}} = -.1495.$$

The reader can verify that the value of the test statistic from Equation 6.1 is $Z = -2.40$, which has a left-tail P-value of .0082 from Table A. The data do support the research hypothesis that there is a significant negative association between debriefing type and instruction form. This conclusion agrees with that obtained for the actual data.

The τ_c coefficient from Equation 6.11 is

$$\tau_c = \frac{4[68(42) - 52(103)]}{265^2} = -.1424.$$

The Goodman-Kruskal or Yule's Q coefficient from Equation 6.12 is

$$\gamma = \frac{68(42) - 52(103)}{68(42) + 52(103)} = -.3044,$$

and the Somers's d coefficients from Equations 6.13 and 6.14 are

$$d_{BA} = \frac{2[68(42) - 52(103)]}{265^2 - 120^2 - 145^2} = -.1437$$

and

$$d_{AB} = \frac{2[68(42) - 52(103)]}{265^2 - 171^2 - 94^2} = -.1555.$$

The SAS and SPSSX solutions to Example 6.3 are shown in Figures 6.4 and 6.5. The values of all descriptive measures of association agree with ours in each case.

```
OPTIONS LINESIZE=80;
CMS FILEDEF RAWIN DISK EX6.3 DATA   A1  ;
DATA A;
INFILE RAWIN;
INPUT A B  FREQ;
  LABEL A = 'INSTRUCTION'
        B = 'DEBRIEFING';
PROC FREQ DATA=A;
 TABLES A*B/ MEASURES;
 WEIGHT FREQ;
RUN;
```

TABLE OF A BY B

A(INSTRUCTION)   B(DEBRIEFING)

```
FREQUENCY |
  PERCENT |
  ROW PCT |
  COL PCT |    1 |    2 |  TOTAL
 - - - - -|- - - -|- - - -|
        1 |   68 |   52 |   120
          | 25.66 | 19.62 | 45.28
          | 56.67 | 43.33 |
          | 39.77 | 55.32 |
 - - - - -|- - - -|- - - -|
        2 |  103 |   42 |   145
          | 38.87 | 15.85 | 54.72
          | 71.03 | 28.97 |
          | 60.23 | 44.68 |
 - - - - -|- - - -|- - - -|
   TOTAL     171      94     265
            64.53   35.47  100.00
```

continued

```
STATISTICS FOR TABLE OF A BY B

STATISTIC                          VALUE        ASE
- - - - - - - - - - - - - - - - - - - - - - - - - - - - - -
GAMMA                              -0.304       0.118
KENDALL'S TAU-B                    -0.149       0.061
STUART'S TAU-C                     -0.142       0.058

SOMERS' D C|R                      -0.144       0.059
SOMERS' D R|C                      -0.156       0.063

PEARSON CORRELATION                -0.149       0.061
SPEARMAN CORRELATION               -0.149       0.061

LAMBDA ASYMMETRIC C|R               0.000       0.000
LAMBDA ASYMMETRIC R|C               0.083       0.077
LAMBDA SYMMETRIC                    0.047       0.044

UNCERTAINTY COEFFICIENT C|R         0.017       0.014
UNCERTAINTY COEFFICIENT R|C         0.016       0.013
UNCERTAINTY COEFFICIENT SYM         0.017       0.014


ESTIMATES OF THE RELATIVE RISK (ROW1/ROW2)

TYPE OF STUDY          VALUE     95% CONFIDENCE BOUNDS
- - - - - - - - - - - - - - - - - - - - - - - - - - - - - -
CASE-CONTROL           0.533     0.321        0.887
COHORT (COL1 RISK)     0.798     0.661        0.963
COHORT (COL2 RISK)     1.496     1.079        2.074

SAMPLE SIZE = 265

ASE IS THE ASYMPTOTIC STANDARD ERROR.
```

Figure 6.4. SAS Solution to Example 6.3

```
data list      /freq 1-5 a 7 b 9
weight by      freq
crosstabs      tables=a by b
options        3,5
STATISTICS     6,7,8,9
begin data
68    1 1
52    1 2
103   2 1
42    2 2
end data
```

A BY B

```
   Count  ┌
   Row Pct│        B
   Tot Pct│                         Row
          │    1  │   2  │  Total
   - - - -│- - - -│- - - -├
     1  │   68  │   52  │   120
        │  56.7 │  43.3 │   45.3
        │  25.7 │  19.6 │
A  - - -│- - - -│- - - -+
     2  │  103  │   42  │   145
        │  71.0 │  29.0 │   54.7
        │  38.9 │  15.8 │
   - - - -│- - -  │ - - - │
   Column    171      94       265
   Total     64.5    35.5     100.0
```

Statistic	Value	ASE1	T-value	Approximate Significance
Kendall's Tau-b	−.14949	.06107	−2.43975	
Kendall's Tau-c	−.14240	.05837	−2.43975	
Gamma	−.30443	.11783	−2.43975	
Somers' D:				
symmetric	−.14937	.06102	−2.43975	
with A dependent	−.15553	.06348	−2.43975	
with B dependent	−.14368	.05887	−2.43975	

Figure 6.5. SPSSX Solution to Example 6.3

7. SUMMARY

This volume has presented several different nonparametric measures of association between two or more variables. Each measure is dimensionless; that is, it can be used when the original variables are measured on different scales.

Spearman's rho and Kendall's tau, covered in Chapter 2, are both appropriate for measuring association between two variables measured on at least an ordinal scale. They generally are not equal to the same value because they measure association in different ways. Rho is equivalent to the Pearson product-moment correlation coefficient with ranks substituted for the values of the variables. Tau is easier to interpret as the proportion of concordant pairs minus the proportion of discordant pairs, and it also has some statistical properties that make it preferable to rho. Both statistics can be used to make inferences about association, as explained in Chapter 3. A similar measure of association among three or more variables is Kendall's coefficient of concordance, covered in Chapter 4. It can be used to make inferences about the agreement among three or more sets of rankings. If there are three or more variables but we want to describe the relationship between only two of the variables when all other variables are held constant, we need to use nonparametric measures of partial correlation, covered in Chapter 5. Nonparametric measures of association for $r \times c$ contingency tables with frequencies on levels representing ordinal measurements were covered in Chapter 6. Tau_b is the most commonly used, but other measures do appear in the literature.

These are just a few of the wide variety of nonparametric measures of association that are available for different types of data and different types of inferences. Some authors call them nonparametric measures of association for ordinal data because they all make use of the order relationships expressed in the data measurements. There are also nonparametric measures of association for nominal data in a contingency table, that is, where the levels of the variables are nominal measurements. These measures are not dependent on the order in which the levels are listed. The reader who wants to learn about other measures should consult Liebetrau (1983), Goodman and Kruskal (1963, 1972, 1980), or Marascuilo and McSweeney (1977).

APPENDIX A: TABLES

TABLE A
Normal Distribution

Table entries are the tail probability, right-tail from the value of Z to plus infinity, and also left tail from minus infinity to the value of $-Z$ for all $P \leq .50$, where Z is the standardized normal variable, $Z = (X - \mu)/\sigma$. Read down the first column to the correct first decimal value of Z, and over to the correct column for the second decimal value. The number at the intersection is the value of P.

Z	.00	.01	.02	.03	.04	.05	.06	.07	.08	.09
0.0	.5000	.4960	.4920	.4880	.4840	.4801	.4761	.4721	.4681	.4641
0.1	.4602	.4562	.4522	.4483	.4443	.4404	.4364	.4325	.4286	.4247
0.2	.4207	.4168	.4129	.4090	.4052	.4013	.3974	.3936	.3897	.3859
0.3	.3821	.3783	.3745	.3707	.3669	.3632	.3594	.3557	.3520	.3483
0.4	.3446	.3409	.3372	.3336	.3300	.3264	.3228	.3192	.3156	.3121
0.5	.3085	.3050	.3015	.2981	.2946	.2912	.2877	.2843	.2810	.2776
0.6	.2743	.2709	.2676	.2643	.2611	.2578	.2546	.2514	.2483	.2451
0.7	.2420	.2389	.2358	.2327	.2296	.2266	.2236	.2206	.2177	.2148
0.8	.2119	.2090	.2061	.2033	.2005	.1977	.1949	.1922	.1894	.1867
0.9	.1841	.1814	.1788	.1762	.1736	.1711	.1685	.1660	.1635	.1611
1.0	.1587	.1562	.1539	.1515	.1492	.1469	.1446	.1423	.1401	.1379
1.1	.1357	.1335	.1314	.1292	.1271	.1251	.1230	.1210	.1190	.1170
1.2	.1151	.1131	.1112	.1093	.1075	.1056	.1038	.1020	.1003	.0985
1.3	.0968	.0951	.0934	.0918	.0901	.0885	.0869	.0853	.0838	.0823
1.4	.0808	.0793	.0778	.0764	.0749	.0735	.0721	.0708	.0694	.0681
1.5	.0668	.0655	.0643	.0630	.0618	.0606	.0594	.0582	.0571	.0559
1.6	.0548	.0537	.0526	.0516	.0505	.0495	.0485	.0475	.0465	.0455
1.7	.0446	.0436	.0427	.0418	.0409	.0401	.0392	.0384	.0375	.0367
1.8	.0359	.0351	.0344	.0336	.0329	.0322	.0314	.0307	.0301	.0294
1.9	.0287	.0281	.0274	.0268	.0262	.0256	.0250	.0244	.0239	.0233
2.0	.0228	.0222	.0217	.0212	.0207	.0202	.0197	.0192	.0188	.0183

continued

TABLE A
Continued

Table entries are the tail probability, right-tail from the value of Z to plus infinity, and also left tail from minus infinity to the value of −Z for all $P \leq .50$, where Z is the standardized normal variable, $Z = (X - \mu)/\sigma$. Read down the first column to the correct first decimal value of Z, and over to the correct column for the second decimal value. The number at the intersection is the value of P.

Z	.00	.01	.02	.03	.04	.05	.06	.07	.08	.09
2.1	.0179	.0174	.0170	.0166	.0162	.0158	.0154	.0150	.0146	.0143
2.2	.0139	.0136	.0132	.0129	.0125	.0122	.0119	.0116	.0113	.0110
2.3	.0107	.0104	.0102	.0099	.0096	.0094	.0091	.0089	.0087	.0084
2.4	.0082	.0080	.0078	.0075	.0073	.0071	.0069	.0068	.0066	.0064
2.5	.0062	.0060	.0059	.0057	.0055	.0054	.0052	.0051	.0049	.0048
2.6	.0047	.0045	.0044	.0043	.0041	.0040	.0039	.0038	.0037	.0036
2.7	.0035	.0034	.0033	.0032	.0031	.0030	.0029	.0028	.0027	.0026
2.8	.0026	.0025	.0024	.0023	.0023	.0022	.0021	.0021	.0020	.0019
2.9	.0019	.0018	.0018	.0017	.0016	.0016	.0015	.0015	.0014	.0014
3.0	.0013	.0013	.0013	.0012	.0012	.0011	.0011	.0011	.0010	.0010
3.1	.0010	.0009	.0009	.0009	.0008	.0008	.0008	.0008	.0007	.0007
3.2	.0007	.0007	.0006	.0006	.0006	.0006	.0006	.0005	.0005	.0005
3.3	.0005	.0005	.0005	.0004	.0004	.0004	.0004	.0004	.0004	.0003
3.4	.0003	.0003	.0003	.0003	.0003	.0003	.0003	.0003	.0003	.0002
3.5	.0002	.0002	.0002	.0002	.0002	.0002	.0002	.0002	.0002	.0002

SOURCE: Adapted from Table V of R. A. Fisher and F. Yates (1963), *Statistical Tables for Biological, Agricultural and Medical Research,* Hafner Publishing Company, New York, with permission of Longman Group Ltd., United Kingdom.

TABLE B
Spearman's Rank Correlation Distribution

Entries labeled P in the table are the cumulative probability, right-tail from the value of r_s to its maximum value 1, for all $r_s \geq 0$, $n \leq 10$. The same probability is a cumulative left-tail probability, from the minimum value -1 to the value $-r_s$. For $10 < n \leq 30$, the table gives the smallest value of r_s (largest value of $-r_s$) for which the right-tail (left-tail) probability for a one-sided test is less than or equal to selected values, .100, .050, .025, .010, .005, .001, shown on the top row. These same values apply to $|r_s|$ for a two-sided test with tail probability .200, .100, .050, .020, .010, .002, shown on the bottom row.

n	r_s	P	n	r_s	P	n	r_s	P	n	r_s	P
3	1.000	.167	7	1.000	.000	8	.810	.011	9	1.000	.000
	.500	.500		.964	.001		.786	.014		.983	.000
4	1.000	.042		.929	.003		.762	.018		.967	.000
	.800	.167		.893	.006		.738	.023		.950	.000
	.600	.208		.857	.012		.714	.029		.933	.000
	.400	.375		.821	.017		.690	.035		.917	.001
	.200	.458		.786	.024		.667	.042		.900	.001
	.000	.542		.750	.033		.643	.048		.883	.002
5	1.000	.008		.714	.044		.619	.057		.867	.002
	.900	.042		.679	.055		.595	.066		.850	.003
	.800	.067		.643	.069		.571	.076		.833	.004
	.700	.117		.607	.083		.548	.085		.817	.005
	.600	.175		.571	.100		.524	.098		.800	.007
	.500	.225		.536	.118		.500	.108		.783	.009
	.400	.258		.500	.133		.476	.122		.767	.011
	.300	.342		.464	.151		.452	.134		.750	.013
	.200	.392		.429	.177		.429	.150		.733	.016
	.100	.475		.393	.198		.405	.163		.717	.018
	.000	.525		.357	.222		.381	.180		.700	.022
6	1.000	.001		.321	.249		.357	.195		.683	.025
	.943	.008		.286	.278		.333	.214		.667	.029
	.886	.017		.250	.297		.310	.231		.650	.033
	.829	.029		.214	.331		.286	.250		.633	.038
	.771	.051		.179	.357		.262	.268		.617	.043
	.714	.068		.143	.391		.238	.291		.600	.048
	.657	.088		.107	.420		.214	.310		.583	.054
	.600	.121		.071	.453		.190	.332		.567	.060
	.543	.149		.036	.482		.167	.352		.550	.066
	.486	.178		.000	.518		.143	.376		.533	.074
	.429	.210	8	1.000	.000		.119	.397		.517	.081
	.371	.249		.976	.000		.095	.420		.500	.089
	.314	.282		.952	.001		.071	.441		.483	.097
	.257	.329		.929	.001		.048	.467		.467	.106
	.200	.357		.905	.002		.024	.488		.450	.115
	.143	.401		.881	.004		.000	.512		.433	.125
	.086	.460		.857	.005					.417	.135
	.029	.500		.833	.008					.400	.146

continued

TABLE B
Continued

n	r_s	P	n	r_s	P	n	r_s	P	n	r_s	P
9	.383	.156	10	.964	.000	10	.636	.027	10	.309	.193
	.367	.168		.952	.000		.624	.030		.297	.203
	.350	.179		.939	.000		.612	.033		.285	.214
	.333	.193		.927	.000		.600	.037		.273	.224
	.317	.205		.915	.000		.588	.040		.261	.235
	.300	.218		.903	.000		.576	.044		.248	.246
	.283	.231		.891	.001		.564	.048		.236	.257
	.267	.247		.879	.001		.552	.052		.224	.268
	.250	.260		.867	.001		.539	.057		.212	.280
	.233	.276		.855	.001		.527	.062		.200	.292
	.217	.290		.842	.002		.515	.067		.188	.304
	.200	.307		.830	.002		.503	.072		.176	.316
	.183	.322		.818	.003		.491	.077		.164	.328
	.167	.339		.806	.004		.479	.083		.152	.341
	.150	.354		.794	.004		.467	.089		.139	.354
	.133	.372		.782	.005		.455	.096		.127	.367
	.117	.388		.770	.007		.442	.102		.115	.379
	.100	.405		.758	.008		.430	.109		.103	.393
	.083	.422		.745	.009		.418	.116		.091	.406
	.067	.440		.733	.010		.406	.124		.079	.419
	.050	.456		.721	.012		.394	.132		.067	.433
	.033	.474		.709	.013		.382	.139		.055	.446
	.017	.491		.697	.015		.370	.148		.042	.459
	.000	.509		.685	.017		.358	.156		.030	.473
10	1.000	.000		.673	.019		.345	.165		.018	.486
	.988	.000		.661	.022		.333	.174		.006	.500
	.976	.000		.648	.025		.321	.184			

continued

TABLE B
Continued

	Right-Tail (Left-Tail) Probability on $r_s(-r_s)$ *for One-Sided Test*					
n	.100	.050	.025	.010	.005	.001
11	.427	.536	.618	.709	.764	.855
12	.406	.503	.587	.678	.734	.825
13	.385	.484	.560	.648	.703	.797
14	.367	.464	.538	.626	.679	.771
15	.354	.446	.521	.604	.657	.750
16	.341	.429	.503	.585	.635	.729
17	.329	.414	.488	.566	.618	.711
18	.317	.401	.474	.550	.600	.692
19	.309	.391	.460	.535	.584	.675
20	.299	.380	.447	.522	.570	.660
21	.292	.370	.436	.509	.556	.647
22	.284	.361	.425	.497	.544	.633
23	.278	.353	.416	.486	.532	.620
24	.275	.344	.407	.476	.521	.608
25	.265	.337	.398	.466	.511	.597
26	.260	.331	.390	.457	.501	.586
27	.255	.324	.383	.449	.492	.576
28	.250	.318	.376	.441	.483	.567
29	.245	.312	.369	.433	.475	.557
30	.241	.307	.363	.426	.467	.548
	.200	.100	.050	.020	.010	.002

Tail Probability on $|r_s|$ *for Two-Sided Test*

For $n > 30$, the probabilities are found from Table A by calculating $Z = r_s\sqrt{n-1}$. The left- or right-tail probability for r_s can be approximated by the left- or right-tail probability for Z, respectively.

SOURCE: The first part of this table ($n \leq 10$) is adapted from Table 2 of M. G. Kendall and J. D. Gibbons (1990), *Rank Correlation Methods* (5th ed.), Edward Arnold, United Kingdom, with permission of Hodder & Stoughton Ltd., United Kingdom. The second part ($10 < n \leq 30$) is adapted from G. J. Glasser and R. F. Winter (1961), "Critical values of the rank correlation coefficient for testing the hypothesis of independence," *Biometrika* 48: 444-448, with permission of the editor of Biometrika Auxiliary Publications and the authors.

TABLE C
Kendall's Tau Distribution

Entries labeled P in the table are the cumulative probability, right tail from the value of τ to its maximum value 1, for all $\tau \geq 0$, $n \leq 10$. The same probability is a cumulative left-tail probability, from the minimum value -1 to the value $-\tau$. For $10 < n \leq 30$, the table gives the smallest value of τ (largest value of $-\tau$) for which the right-tail (left-tail) probability for a one-sided test is less than or equal to selected values, .100, .050, .025, .010, .005, shown on the top row. These same values apply to $|\tau|$ for a two-sided test with tail probability .200, .100, .050, .020, .010, shown on the bottom row.

n	τ	P	n	τ	P	n	τ	P	n	τ	P
3	1.000	.167	7	1.000	.000	9	1.000	.000	10	1.000	.000
	.333	.500		.905	.001		.944	.000		.956	.000
4	1.000	.042		.810	.005		.889	.000		.911	.000
	.667	.167		.714	.015		.833	.000		.867	.000
	.333	.375		.619	.035		.778	.001		.822	.000
	.000	.625		.524	.068		.722	.003		.778	.000
5	1.000	.008		.429	.119		.667	.006		.733	.001
	.800	.042		.333	.191		.611	.012		.689	.002
	.600	.117		.238	.281		.556	.022		.644	.005
	.400	.242		.143	.386		.500	.038		.600	.008
	.200	.408		.048	.500		.444	.060		.556	.014
	.000	.592	8	1.000	.000		.389	.090		.511	.023
6	1.000	.001		.929	.000		.333	.130		.467	.036
	.867	.008		.857	.001		.278	.179		.422	.054
	.733	.028		.786	.003		.222	.238		.378	.078
	.600	.068		.714	.007		.167	.306		.333	.108
	.467	.136		.643	.016		.111	.381		.289	.146
	.333	.235		.571	.031		.056	.460		.244	.190
	.200	.360		.500	.054		.000	.540		.200	.242
	.067	.500		.429	.089					.156	.300
				.357	.138					.111	.364
				.286	.199					.067	.431
				.214	.274					.022	.500
				.143	.360						
				.071	.452						
				.000	.548						

continued

TABLE C
Continued

n	Right-Tail (Left-Tail) Probability on τ (−τ) for One-Sided Test				
	.100	.050	.025	.010	.005
11	.345	.418	.491	.564	.600
12	.303	.394	.455	.545	.576
13	.308	.359	.436	.513	.564
14	.275	.363	.407	.473	.516
15	.276	.333	.390	.467	.505
16	.250	.317	.383	.433	.483
17	.250	.309	.368	.426	.471
18	.242	.294	.346	.412	.451
19	.228	.287	.333	.392	.439
20	.221	.274	.326	.379	.421
21	.210	.267	.314	.371	.410
22	.203	.264	.307	.359	.394
23	.202	.257	.296	.352	.391
24	.196	.246	.290	.341	.377
25	.193	.240	.287	.333	.367
26	.188	.237	.280	.329	.360
27	.179	.231	.271	.322	.356
28	.180	.228	.265	.312	.344
29	.172	.222	.261	.310	.340
30	.172	.218	.255	.301	.333
	.200	.100	.050	.020	.010
	Tail probability on |τ| for Two-Sided Test				

For $n > 30$, the probabilities are found from Table A by calculating $Z = 3\tau\sqrt{n(n-1)}/\sqrt{2(2n+5)}$. The left- or right-tail probability for τ can be approximated by the left- or right-tail probability for Z, respectively.

SOURCE: The first part of this table ($n \leq 10$) is adapted from Table 1 of M. G. Kendall and J. D. Gibbons (1990), *Rank Correlation Methods* (5th ed.), Edward Arnold, United Kingdom, with permission of Hodder & Stoughton Ltd., United Kingdom. The second part ($10 < n \leq 30$) is adapted from L. Kaarsemaker and A. van Wijngaarden (1953), "Tables for use in rank correlation," *Statistica Neerlandica* 7: 41-54, with permission of the publisher.

TABLE D
Kendall's Coefficient of Concordance Distribution

Entries labeled P in the table are the cumulative probability, right-tail from the value of S to its maximum value, for all $P \le .50$, $k \le 8$ for $n = 3$, $k \le 4$ for $n = 4$, and $k = 3$ for $n = 5$.

n	k	S	P	n	k	S	P	n	k	S	P	n	k	S	P
3	2	8	.167	3	7	98	.000	4	2	20	.042	4	4	80	.000
		6	.500			96	.000			18	.167			78	.001
	3	18	.028			86	.000			16	.208			76	.001
		14	.194			78	.001			14	.375			74	.001
		8	.361			74	.003			12	.458			72	.002
	4	32	.005			72	.004		3	45	.002			70	.003
		26	.042			62	.008			43	.002			68	.003
		24	.069			56	.016			41	.017			66	.006
		18	.125			54	.021			37	.033			64	.007
		14	.273			50	.027			35	.054			62	.012
		8	.431			42	.051			33	.075			58	.014
	5	50	.001			38	.085			29	.148			56	.019
		42	.008			32	.112			27	.175			54	.033
		38	.024			26	.192			25	.207			52	.036
		32	.039			24	.237			21	.300			50	.052
		26	.093			18	.305			19	.342			48	.054
		24	.124			14	.486			17	.446			46	.068
		18	.182		8	128	.000							44	.077
		14	.367			126	.000							42	.094
	6	72	.000			122	.000							40	.105
		62	.002			114	.000							38	.141
		56	.006			104	.000							36	.158
		54	.008			98	.001							34	.190
		50	.012			96	.001							32	.200
		42	.029			86	.002							30	.242
		38	.052			78	.005							26	.324
		32	.072			74	.008							24	.355
		26	.142			72	.010							22	.389
		24	.184			62	.018							20	.432
		18	.252			56	.030									
		14	.430			54	.038									
						50	.047								
						42	.079								
						38	.120								
						32	.149								
						26	.236								
						24	.285								
						18	.355								

continued

TABLE D
Continued

Entries labeled P in the table are the cumulative probability, right-tail from the value of S to its maximum value, for all $P \leq .50$, $k \leq 8$ for $n = 3$, $k \leq 4$ for $n = 4$, and $k = 3$ for $n = 5$.

n	k	S	P	n	k	S	P
5	3	90	.000	5	3	56	.096
		86	.001			54	.117
		82	.003			52	.127
		80	.004			50	.163
		78	.005			48	.172
		76	.008			46	.213
		74	.015			44	.236
		72	.017			42	.253
		70	.026			40	.291
		68	.028			38	.326
		66	.038			36	.347
		64	.045			34	.406
		62	.056			32	.432
		60	.063			30	.475
		58	.080			28	.493

For n and k outside the range of this table, P-values are found as a right-tail probability from Table E with $n - 1$ degrees of freedom for the test statistic

$$Q = \frac{12S}{kn(n + 1)}.$$

SOURCE: Adapted from Table 5 of M. G. Kendall and J. D. Gibbons (1990), *Rank Correlation Methods* (5th ed.), Edward Arnold, United Kingdom, with permission of Hodder & Stoughton Ltd., United Kingdom.

TABLE E
Chi-Square Distribution

Table entries on all df lines are the values of a chi-square random variable for which the right-tail probability is as given on the top row.

Right-Tail Probability

df	.99	.98	.95	.90	.80	.70	.50	.30	.20	.10	.05	.02	.01	.001
1	.00016	.00063	.0039	.016	.064	.15	.46	1.07	1.64	2.71	3.84	5.41	6.64	10.83
2	.02	.04	.10	.21	.45	.71	1.39	2.41	3.22	4.60	5.99	7.82	9.21	13.82
3	.12	.18	.35	.58	1.00	1.42	2.37	3.66	4.64	6.25	7.82	9.84	11.34	16.27
4	.30	.43	.71	1.06	1.65	2.20	3.36	4.88	5.99	7.78	9.49	11.67	13.28	18.46
5	.55	.75	1.14	1.61	2.34	3.00	4.35	6.06	7.29	9.24	11.07	13.39	15.09	20.52
6	.87	1.13	1.64	2.20	3.07	3.83	5.35	7.23	8.56	10.64	12.59	15.03	16.81	22.46
7	1.24	1.56	2.17	2.83	3.82	4.67	6.35	8.38	9.80	12.02	14.07	16.62	18.48	24.32
8	1.65	2.03	2.73	3.49	4.59	5.53	7.34	9.52	11.03	13.36	15.51	18.17	20.09	26.12
9	2.09	2.53	3.32	4.17	5.38	6.39	8.34	10.66	12.24	14.68	16.92	19.68	21.67	27.88
10	2.56	3.06	3.94	4.86	6.18	7.27	9.34	11.78	13.44	15.99	18.31	21.16	23.21	29.59
11	3.05	3.61	4.58	5.58	6.99	8.15	10.34	12.90	14.63	17.28	19.68	22.62	24.72	31.26
12	3.57	4.18	5.23	6.30	7.81	9.03	11.34	14.01	15.81	18.55	21.03	24.05	26.22	32.91
13	4.11	4.76	5.89	7.04	8.63	9.93	12.34	15.12	16.98	19.81	22.36	25.47	27.69	34.53
14	4.66	5.37	6.57	7.79	9.47	10.82	13.34	16.22	18.15	21.06	23.68	26.87	29.14	36.12
15	5.23	5.98	7.26	8.55	10.31	11.72	14.34	17.32	19.31	22.31	25.00	28.26	30.58	37.70
16	5.81	6.61	7.96	9.31	11.15	12.62	15.34	18.42	20.46	23.54	26.30	29.63	32.00	39.29
17	6.41	7.26	8.67	10.08	12.00	13.53	16.34	19.51	21.62	24.77	27.59	31.00	33.41	40.75
18	7.02	7.91	9.39	10.86	12.86	14.44	17.34	20.60	22.76	25.99	28.87	32.35	34.80	42.31
19	7.63	8.57	10.12	11.65	13.72	15.35	18.34	21.69	23.90	27.20	30.14	33.69	36.19	43.82
20	8.26	9.24	10.85	12.44	14.58	16.27	19.34	22.78	25.04	28.41	31.41	35.02	37.57	45.32

Table entries on all df lines are the values of a chi-square random variable for which the right-tail probability is as given on the top row.

Right-Tail Probability

df	.99	.98	.95	.90	.80	.70	.50	.30	.20	.10	.05	.02	.01	.001
21	8.90	9.92	11.59	13.24	15.44	17.18	20.34	23.86	26.17	29.62	32.67	36.34	38.93	46.80
22	9.54	10.60	12.34	14.04	16.31	18.10	21.34	24.94	27.30	30.81	33.92	37.66	40.29	48.27
23	10.20	11.29	13.09	14.85	17.19	19.02	22.34	26.02	28.43	32.01	35.17	38.97	41.64	49.73
24	10.86	11.99	13.85	15.66	18.06	19.94	23.34	27.10	29.55	33.20	36.42	40.27	42.98	51.18
25	11.52	12.70	14.61	16.47	18.94	20.87	24.34	28.17	30.68	34.38	37.65	41.57	44.31	52.62
26	12.20	13.41	15.38	17.29	19.82	21.79	25.34	29.25	31.80	35.56	38.88	42.86	45.64	54.05
27	12.88	14.12	16.15	18.11	20.70	22.72	26.34	30.32	32.91	36.74	40.11	44.14	46.96	55.48
28	13.56	14.85	16.93	18.94	21.59	23.65	27.34	31.39	34.03	37.92	41.34	45.42	48.28	56.89
29	14.26	15.57	17.71	19.77	22.48	24.58	28.34	32.46	35.14	39.09	42.56	46.69	49.59	58.30
30	14.95	16.31	18.49	20.60	23.36	25.51	29.34	33.53	36.25	40.26	43.77	47.96	50.89	59.70

For df > 30, the probabilities based on the asymptotic distribution are approximated as follows:

Let Q be a chi-square random variable with degrees of freedom df. A right- or left-tail probability for Q is approximated by a right- or left-tail probability, respectively, from Table A for Z, where

$$Z = \sqrt{2Q} - \sqrt{2(df)} - 1 .$$

SOURCE: Adapted from Table IV of R. A. Fisher and F. Yates (1963), *Statistical Tables for Biological, Agricultural and Medical Research*, Hafner Publishing Company, New York, with permission of Longman Group Ltd., United Kingdom.

TABLE F
Critical Values of $\tau_{XY.Z}$
(for Kendall's Partial Rank Correlation Coefficient)

n	.05	One-Tailed Level of Significance .025	.01	.005
3	1	1	1	1
4	0.707	1	1	1
5	0.667	0.802	0.816	1
6	0.600	0.667	0.764	0.866
7	0.527	0.617	0.712	0.761
8	0.484	0.565	0.648	0.713
9	0.443	0.515	0.602	0.660
10	0.413	0.480	0.562	0.614
11	0.387	0.453	0.530	0.581
12	0.365	0.430	0.505	0.548
13	0.347	0.410	0.481	0.527
14	0.331	0.391	0.458	0.503
15	0.317	0.375	0.439	0.482
16	0.305	0.361	0.423	0.466
17	0.294	0.348	0.410	0.450
18	0.284	0.336	0.395	0.434
19	0.275	0.326	0.382	0.421
20	0.267	0.317	0.372	0.410
25	0.235	0.278	0.328	0.362
30	0.211	0.251	0.297	0.328

SOURCE: Adapted from S. Maghsoodloo (1975), "Estimates of the quantiles of Kendall's partial rank correlation coefficient and additional quantile estimates," *Journal of Statistical Computation and Simulation* 4: 155-164; and S. Maghsoodloo and L. L. Pallos (1981), "Asymptotic behavior of Kendall's partial rank correlation coefficient and additional quantile estimates," *Journal of Statistical Computation and Simulation* 13: 41-48; with permission of Gordon and Breach Science Publishers Inc.

APPENDIX B: FURTHER READING

BRADLEY, J. V. (1968) Distribution-Free Statistical Tests. Englewood Cliffs, NJ: Prentice-Hall.

CONOVER, W. J. (1980) Practical Nonparametric Statistics. New York: John Wiley.

DANIEL, W. (1990) Applied Nonparametric Statistics. Boston: PWS-Kent.

FRIEDMAN, M. (1937) "The use of ranks to avoid the assumption of normality implicit in the analysis of variance." Journal of the American Statistical Association 32: 675-701.

GIBBONS, J. D. (1985) Nonparametric Methods for Quantitative Analysis (2nd ed.). Syracuse, NY: American Sciences Press.

GIBBONS, J. D. (1992) Nonparametric Statistics: An Introduction. Sage University Paper series on Quantitative Applications in the Social Sciences, 07-090. Newbury Park, CA: Sage.

GIBBONS, J. D., and CHAKRABORTI, S. (1992) Nonparametric Statistical Inference (3rd ed.). New York: Marcel Dekker.

KENDALL, M. G., and GIBBONS, J. D. (1980) Rank Correlation Methods (5th ed.). London: Edward Arnold.

KRUSKAL, W. H. (1958). "Ordinal measures of association." Journal of the American Statistical Association 53: 814-861.

LEACH, C. (1979) Introduction to Statistics: A Nonparametric Approach for the Social Sciences. New York: John Wiley.

LIEBETRAU, A. M. (1983) Measures of Association. Beverly Hills, CA: Sage.

MARASCUILO, L. A., and McSWEENEY, M. (1977) Nonparametric and Distribution-Free Methods for the Social Sciences. Monterey, CA: Brooks/Cole.

SIEGEL, S., and CASTELLAN, N. J. (1988) Nonparametric Statistics for the Behavioral Sciences (2nd ed.). New York: McGraw-Hill.

SOMERS, R. H. (1962) "A new asymmetric measure of association for ordinal variables." American Sociological Review 27: 799-811.

SPEARMAN, C. (1904) "The proof and measurement of association between two things." American Journal of Psychology 15: 72-101.

STUART, A. (1953) "The estimation and comparison of strengths of association in contingency tables." Biometrika 40: 105-110.

REFERENCES

CANCIAN, F. M., and ROSS, B. L. (1981) "Mass media and the women's movement: 1900-1977." Journal of Applied Behavioral Science 17: 9-26.

CHARLOP, M. H., and CARLSON, J. (1983) "Reversal and nonreversal shifts in autistic children." Journal of Experimental Child Psychology 36: 56-67.

EHRENBERG, A. S. C. (1952) "On sampling from a population of rankers." Biometrika 39: 82-87.

FESTINGER, L., and MACCOBY, N. (1964) "On resistance to persuasive communications." Journal of Abnormal and Social Psychology 68: 359-366.

FISHER, R. A., and YATES, E. (1963) Statistical Tables for Biological, Agricultural and Medical Research. New York: Hafner.

GLASSER, G. J., and WINTER, R. F. (1961) "Critical values of the rank correlation coefficient for testing the hypothesis of independence." Biometrika 48: 444-448.

GOODMAN, L. A., and KRUSKAL, W. H. (1963) "Measures of association for cross-classifications, III: Approximate sampling theory." Journal of the American Statistical Association 58: 310-364.

GOODMAN, L. A., and KRUSKAL, W. H. (1972) "Measures of association for cross-classifications, IV: Simplification of asymptotic variances." Journal of the American Statistical Association 67: 415-421.

GOODMAN, L. A., and KRUSKAL, W. H. (1980) Measures of Association for Cross-Classifications. New York: Springer.

HAYS, W. L. (1960) "A note on average tau as a measure of concordance." Journal of the American Statistical Association 55: 331-341.

HUMPHREYS, A., and SMITH, P. K. (1987) "Rough and tumble, friendship and dominance in school children: Evidence for continuity and change with age." Child Development 58: 201-212.

KAARSEMAKER, L., and VAN WIJNGAARDEN, A. (1953) "Tables for use in rank correlation." Statistica Neerlandica 7: 41-54.

KENDALL, M. G., and GIBBONS, J. D. (1980) Rank Correlation Methods (5th ed.). London: Edward Arnold.

KOHNKEN, G., and MAASS, A. (1985) "Eyewitness testimony: False alarms on biased instructions?" Journal of Applied Psychology 73: 363-370.

LIEBETRAU, A. M. (1983) Measures of Association. Beverly Hills, CA: Sage.

MAGHSOODLOO, S. (1975) "Estimates of the quantiles of Kendall's partial rank correlation coefficient and additional quantile estimates." Journal of Statistical Computation and Simulation 4: 155-164.

MAGHSOODLOO, S., and PALLOS, L. L. (1981) "Asymptotic behavior of Kendall's partial rank correlation coefficient and additional quantile estimates." Journal of Statistical Computation and Simulation 13: 41-48.

MARASCUILO, L. A., and McSWEENEY, M. (1977) Nonparametric and Distribution-Free Methods for the Social Sciences. Monterey, CA: Brooks/Cole.

NELSON, J. E., DUNCAN, C. P., and FRONTCZAK, N. T. (1985) "The distraction hypothesis and radio advertising." Journal of Marketing 49(Winter): 60-71.

RANDALL, D. (1987) "The portrayal of business malfeasance in the elite and general public media." Social Science Quarterly 68: 283-293.

ROBICHAUD, M., and WILSON, W. (1976) "Rank order of preference of blacks and whites." Southern Journal of Education Research 10: 156-166.

RUBENSTEIN, C. (1982) "Regional states of mind." Psychology Today 16(February): 22-30.

SINCLAIR, E., GUTHRIE, D., and FORNESS, S. R. (1984) "Establishing a connection between severity of learning disabilities and classroom attention problems." Journal of Educational Research 78(1): 18-21.

SOMERS, R. H. (1980) "Simple approximations to null sampling variances: Goodman and Kruskal's gamma, Kendall's tau, and Somers's d_{yx}." Sociological Methods & Research 9: 115-126.

STEVENSON, W. B. (1990) "Formal structure and networks of interaction within organizations." Social Science Research 19: 113-131.

WALLIS, W. A., and ROBERTS, H. V. (1956) Statistics: A New Approach. New York: Free Press.

ZELLNER, D. A., HARNER, D. E., and ADLER, R. L. (1989) "Effects of eating abnormalities and gender on perceptions of desirable body shape." Journal of Abnormal Psychology 98: 93-96.

ABOUT THE AUTHOR

JEAN DICKINSON GIBBONS is the Thomas D. Russell Professor of Applied Statistics at the University of Alabama. She earned the Ph.D. degree in statistics from Virginia Polytechnic Institute and State University, after earning the B.A. and M.A. degrees in mathematics from Duke University. She was an Associate Professor of Statistics at the Wharton School of the University of Pennsylvania before taking her present position. She has published several books on nonparametric statistics; some of these are theoretical and some are applied. She has also published numerous articles, which have appeared in the *Journal of the American Statistical Association, The American Statistician,* the *Journal of the* *istical Society,* and the *Journal of Quality Technology,* and g others. She has been a Fellow of the American Statistical Association since 1972 and has been elected to that organization's Board of Directors for four different terms. She has also been active in consulting and contract teaching in nonparametric statistics for the U.S. Army Logistics Management College of the Department of Defense

300.151
G4416

108020

LINCOLN CHRISTIAN COLLEGE AND SEMINARY

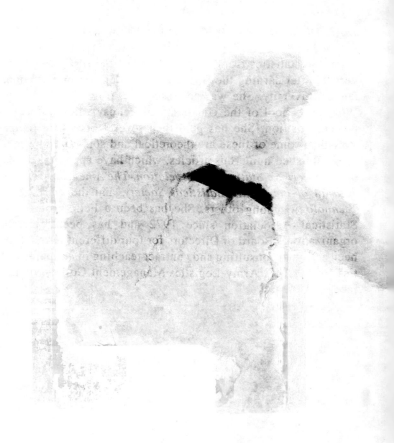